Post-Quantum Cryptography

Securing Data in the Quantum Age

Charles S. Michaelis

Preface

The digital world as we know it is built on a foundation of trust. That trust, in turn, rests on the security of our cryptographic systems. We rely on cryptography to protect our online banking, secure our communications, safeguard our personal data, and ensure the integrity of our digital infrastructure. But what if I told you that this foundation is about to be shaken to its core?

That's the reality we face with the advent of quantum computing. Quantum computers, leveraging the bizarre and powerful principles of quantum mechanics, have the potential to break many of the cryptographic algorithms that underpin our digital world. Algorithms like RSA and ECC, which have protected our data for decades, will become vulnerable. This isn't science fiction; it's a looming reality.

(Personal Connection): I've been fascinated by cryptography and cybersecurity for years. The elegance of the mathematics, the constant battle between code makers and code breakers, and the profound impact on our society have always captivated me. When I first learned about the threat posed by quantum computing, I knew I had to delve deeper. This book is the culmination of that journey – a journey of exploration, learning, and a growing sense of urgency.

This book is not intended to be a scare tactic. Instead, I want to say that there is a solution. That's what this book is about: *Post-Quantum Cryptography (PQC)*. PQC is our proactive defense against the quantum threat. It's about developing and deploying new cryptographic algorithms that are believed to be resistant to attacks from both classical and quantum computers. It's about building a more secure and resilient future.

(Why This Book?):

I wrote this book because I believe that understanding PQC is essential for *everyone* involved in cybersecurity, from seasoned professionals to students just starting their careers. The transition to PQC will be a complex and challenging undertaking, and it will require a collective effort. My goal is to demystify PQC, making it accessible to a wide audience and empowering readers to take action.

(What You'll Learn):

This book is designed to be a comprehensive and practical guide to PQC. We'll start with the fundamentals, explaining the threat posed by quantum computing and the basic principles of PQC. We'll then dive deep into the leading PQC algorithms, exploring their underlying mathematics, security properties, and performance characteristics. We'll also cover the practical aspects of implementing PQC, including integration with existing systems, migration strategies, and testing and validation. Finally, we'll look ahead to the future of cybersecurity in the quantum age, discussing the ongoing challenges and ethical considerations.

I've made a conscious effort to write this book in a conversational and accessible style. I've avoided unnecessary jargon and complex mathematical formulas wherever possible. My aim is to explain complex concepts in a clear and intuitive way, using analogies and real-world examples to illustrate the key points.

Who This Book Is For:

This book is for anyone who wants to understand the quantum threat and how to protect their data and systems in the quantum age. Whether you're a:

- Cybersecurity professional
- Software developer
- IT manager
- Student
- Researcher
- Or simply someone curious about the future of cybersecurity

…this book will provide you with the knowledge and skills you need to navigate the complex landscape of PQC.

The quantum age is coming, and it's time to prepare. This book is your guide to that preparation. It's a call to action, urging you to take the quantum threat seriously and to start planning your transition to PQC. The future of cybersecurity depends on it. Let's embrace this challenge with confidence, vigilance, and a commitment to building a more secure and resilient digital world.

Table of Contents

Part I: Understanding the Quantum Threat

Chapter 1: Introduction: Cybersecurity in the Quantum Age

Imagine this: You wake up one morning to discover that your online bank account has been emptied, your encrypted medical records have been leaked, and your company's confidential trade secrets are plastered all over the internet. What happened? A sophisticated phishing attack? A zero-day exploit? Perhaps. But what if the culprit was something far more profound – something that renders the very foundations of our current cybersecurity defenses obsolete? That something is the rise of quantum computing.

(1.1: The Quantum Computing Revolution: A New Cybersecurity Paradigm)

So, when we talk about a "revolution," it's not just about faster processors or smaller devices. It's a fundamental shift in how we think about computation itself. Classical computers, the ones we use every day, operate using bits – 0s and 1s. Think of it like a light switch: it's either on or off. But quantum computers, on the other hand, leverage qubits. A qubit isn't just an on or off switch; it's a dimmer switch that can be *both* on *and* off *simultaneously*. This is the magic of *superposition*.

Now, imagine you're trying to find a specific grain of sand on a beach. A classical computer would have to check each grain, one by one. But a quantum computer, using superposition, can effectively look at *all* the grains of sand *at the same time*. This is an oversimplification, of course, but it gives you a sense of the potential for massive parallel computation.

Personal Perspective: I've always been fascinated by the concept of parallel processing. But the scale of parallelism offered by quantum computing is mind-boggling. It's like going from a single chef in a kitchen to an army of chefs, all working simultaneously on different parts of the same dish.

But superposition is only half the story. The other key ingredient is *entanglement*. When two qubits are entangled, their fates are intertwined, regardless of the distance separating them. Measuring the state of one qubit instantaneously reveals the state of the other. Einstein famously called this "spooky action at a distance."

Entanglement allows quantum computers to perform complex calculations that are simply impossible for classical computers. This is where algorithms like Shor's algorithm come into play. Shor's algorithm, as we discussed, is a quantum algorithm that can factor large numbers exponentially faster than the best-known classical algorithms. And that's what makes it so dangerous to our current cryptographic systems.

(Relating it to Cybersecurity): Why does this matter to cybersecurity? Because our current public-key cryptography relies on the fact that factoring large numbers is a computationally hard problem for classical computers. If a quantum computer can factor large numbers quickly, it can break RSA, which is the foundation of much of our online security.

This isn't just a theoretical threat. As quantum computers continue to develop, the risk of a quantum attack on our cryptographic infrastructure becomes more real. It's like a slow-moving train wreck: we can see it coming, and we need to take action to mitigate the damage.

Now, let's talk about what this "new cybersecurity paradigm" actually means. It's not just about replacing our existing cryptographic algorithms with quantum-resistant ones. It's about rethinking our entire approach to security. It's about:

- **Adopting a "quantum-first" mindset:** Considering the quantum threat in all aspects of our security planning and implementation.
- **Implementing defense-in-depth strategies:** Relying on multiple layers of security to protect our data.
- **Staying informed about the latest developments in PQC:** The field of post-quantum cryptography is constantly evolving, and we need to stay up-to-date on the latest research and best practices.
- **Collaborating and sharing information:** The quantum threat is a shared challenge, and we need to work together to develop and deploy effective solutions.

In essence, the quantum computing revolution demands a paradigm shift in cybersecurity. We need to move from a reactive approach – patching vulnerabilities after they're discovered – to a proactive approach – anticipating and mitigating threats before they materialize. We need to embrace the challenge and prepare for the quantum age with confidence and vigilance.

And that's what this book is all about. It's about empowering you with the knowledge and skills you need to navigate this new landscape and secure your data for the future.

(1.2: Why Current Cryptography Fails Against Quantum Attacks)

Imagine building a fortress out of carefully stacked stones. It looks strong, impressive even. But what if a new type of earthquake comes along that exploits the fundamental weaknesses in the design – weaknesses that were never apparent before? That's essentially what quantum computers do to our current cryptographic "fortresses."

The core issue boils down to the mathematical problems upon which our most widely used cryptographic algorithms are built. These problems, for classical computers, are incredibly difficult to solve in a reasonable timeframe. That's why they've been the bedrock of secure communication for decades. We're talking about algorithms like RSA (Rivest-Shamir-Adleman), ECC (Elliptic Curve Cryptography), and Diffie-Hellman.

RSA relies on the difficulty of factoring large numbers. If you give me two massive prime numbers, multiplying them together is easy. But if I give you the product of those two primes, finding the original prime numbers becomes exponentially harder as the numbers get larger. That computational asymmetry is the heart of RSA's security.

ECC is similar, but relies on the difficulty of solving the *discrete logarithm problem* on elliptic curves. Elliptic curves are complex mathematical curves with fascinating properties. Again, performing the forward operation is relatively easy, but reversing it – finding the discrete logarithm – is incredibly difficult for classical computers. ECC has become particularly popular for mobile devices and other resource-constrained environments due to its smaller key sizes compared to RSA.

Diffie-Hellman is a key exchange protocol that allows two parties to establish a shared secret key over an insecure channel. It's also based on the difficulty of the discrete logarithm problem.

So, what's the quantum earthquake that shatters these foundations? It's *Shor's algorithm*.

Shor's algorithm, developed by Peter Shor in 1994, is a quantum algorithm that can factor large numbers and solve the discrete logarithm problem exponentially faster than the best-known classical algorithms. This is a game-changer.

Personal Perspective: When I first studied Shor's algorithm, I was struck by its elegance and sheer power. It felt like discovering a secret weapon that could unlock all the secrets of the digital world. But with that power comes a great responsibility to understand its implications and develop defenses.

Let's try to understand, at a high level, *why* Shor's algorithm is so effective. It leverages the quantum properties of superposition and quantum Fourier transform to efficiently find the period of a mathematical function. Finding the period allows you to then deduce the prime factors of the number you're trying to factor, or solve the discrete logarithm problem.

I won't bore you with the complex math (we'll save that for the appendices, perhaps!), but the key takeaway is that Shor's algorithm transforms a problem that is exponentially hard for classical computers into a problem that is polynomially solvable for quantum computers. That's the difference between taking billions of years to solve a problem and solving it in a matter of minutes.

What are the practical consequences?

- **RSA is Broken:** A quantum computer running Shor's algorithm can efficiently factor the large numbers used in RSA encryption, allowing it to decrypt RSA-encrypted messages and forge digital signatures.
- **ECC is Broken:** Similarly, a quantum computer can efficiently solve the discrete logarithm problem on elliptic curves, breaking ECC encryption and compromising key exchange protocols.
- **Diffie-Hellman is Broken:** The same fate awaits Diffie-Hellman key exchange, as it's also vulnerable to Shor's algorithm.

It's important to note that *symmetric-key cryptography*, like AES (Advanced Encryption Standard), isn't directly broken by Shor's algorithm. However, quantum computers can still speed up brute-force attacks on symmetric keys using *Grover's algorithm*. Grover's algorithm provides a quadratic speedup, meaning it reduces the search space from N to the square root of N. This effectively halves the key length. So, AES-128 becomes equivalent to AES-64, which is considered insecure. To mitigate this, we can simply increase the key size. AES-256 is generally considered to be quantum-resistant for the foreseeable future.

This brings up a critical point: The impact of quantum computers is *asymmetric*. Public-key cryptography is fundamentally compromised, while symmetric-key cryptography requires only a relatively minor adjustment (increasing key sizes).

(Code Example Preparation - Setting the Stage):

While we can't demonstrate Shor's algorithm with readily available code (simulating quantum computers is incredibly resource-intensive!), we can illustrate the *impact* of factoring on RSA.

```python
    # This is a conceptual example ONLY. It's not
feasible to factor large RSA keys with this code.

def is_prime(n):
  """Simple primality test (for demonstration purposes
only)."""
  if n <= 1:
    return False
  for i in range(2, int(n**0.5) + 1):
    if n % i == 0:
      return False
  return True

def factorize(n):
  """Naive factorization (for demonstration purposes
only)."""
  for i in range(2, n):
    if n % i == 0:
      return i, n // i  # Returns two factors
  return None, None  # Not factorable

# Simulate a "small" RSA key
p = 61 # A prime number
q = 53 # Another prime number
n = p * q  # The public key (modulus)
```

```
print(f"Public Key (n): {n}")

#Imagine an attacker can somehow "factorize" n.
factor1, factor2 = factorize(n)

if factor1 and factor2:
  print(f"Factors found: {factor1}, {factor2}")
  print("RSA is compromised (in this simplified example)")
else:
  print("Could not factorize (as expected with large RSA
keys and classical computers)")
```

(Explanation of the Code):

This code provides a *simplified* illustration of RSA factorization. Please understand that *this code cannot factor real-world RSA keys*. It's purely for demonstration. A real-world implementation would require far more sophisticated algorithms and computational power.

The is_prime function checks if a number is prime (again, for illustrative purposes only). The factorize function attempts to find two factors of a given number. The code then simulates the creation of a small RSA key by multiplying two prime numbers together. If the factorize function can successfully find the factors, it demonstrates the principle of how RSA can be broken if factorization becomes easy.

(Important Disclaimer):

This code is for educational purposes only and should NOT be used for any real-world cryptographic applications. It is vulnerable to numerous attacks and is not secure.

The point of this exercise is to illustrate the fundamental weakness of RSA: if an attacker can factor the modulus, the entire system is compromised. Shor's algorithm provides a way for quantum computers to do just that, making RSA and other vulnerable algorithms obsolete in the quantum age.

This code example provides a tangible link between the theoretical concepts and the practical implications. While it can't fully demonstrate the power of Shor's algorithm, it highlights the vulnerability of RSA to factorization attacks.

(1.3: Post-Quantum Cryptography (PQC): A Proactive Defense)

It's crucial to reiterate: PQC *isn't* about using quantum computers to encrypt data. That's the realm of Quantum Key Distribution (QKD), which we'll touch upon later. PQC is about designing *classical* algorithms that are believed to be secure even against attacks from quantum computers. The aim is to find mathematical problems that are hard for *both* classical and quantum computers.

(Relatable Analogy): Think of it like this: If classical cryptography is based on hiding a secret in a complex maze, PQC is based on hiding a secret inside a mathematical black hole – a region of spacetime from which nothing, not even quantum computers, can escape. (Okay, the black hole analogy is a bit of a stretch, but it conveys the idea of inherent computational difficulty!)

The beauty of PQC is that it allows us to leverage our existing computing infrastructure and security protocols. We don't need to build quantum networks or replace all our classical computers. We simply need to replace the vulnerable cryptographic algorithms with PQC algorithms. Easier said than done, of course, but that's the fundamental concept.

Personal Perspective: What excites me most about PQC is the ingenuity and creativity of the researchers who are developing these algorithms. They're pushing the boundaries of mathematics and computer science to create new and innovative solutions to a very real and pressing problem.

So, what are these new, earthquake-resistant cryptographic algorithms? They fall into several broad categories, each based on different mathematical problems:

- **Lattice-Based Cryptography:** This is currently the most promising family of PQC algorithms. Lattice-based cryptography relies on the difficulty of solving problems on mathematical lattices, which are geometric structures with repeating patterns. The specific problems used in lattice-based cryptography are the Learning With Errors (LWE) problem and the Module Learning With Errors (MLWE) problem. These problems are believed to be hard for both classical and quantum computers. Examples include

CRYSTALS-Kyber (key encapsulation) and CRYSTALS-Dilithium (digital signatures), which were selected by NIST for standardization.

- **Code-Based Cryptography:** Code-based cryptography relies on the difficulty of decoding random linear codes. The most prominent example is Classic McEliece, which is based on the McEliece cryptosystem from 1978. The security of Classic McEliece is based on the difficulty of decoding random Goppa codes, which are a special type of linear code. Classic McEliece was also selected by NIST for standardization.

- **Hash-Based Signatures:** Hash-based signatures are based on the security properties of cryptographic hash functions. The main advantage of hash-based signatures is that they are very simple and well-understood. They also have provable security, meaning that their security can be mathematically proven based on the security of the underlying hash function. The most prominent example is SPHINCS+, which was also selected by NIST for standardization.

- **Multivariate Cryptography:** Multivariate cryptography relies on the difficulty of solving systems of multivariate polynomial equations. This approach has been around for a while, but it has been challenging to design secure and efficient multivariate cryptosystems. Rainbow is a multivariate signature scheme that was a finalist in the NIST PQC competition, but it was not selected for standardization due to security concerns.

- **Isogeny-Based Cryptography:** Isogeny-based cryptography relies on the difficulty of finding isogenies between elliptic curves. An isogeny is a special type of mapping between elliptic curves. Isogeny-based cryptography has some attractive properties, such as small key sizes, but it has also been subject to recent attacks. SIKE (Supersingular Isogeny Key Encapsulation) was a candidate in the NIST PQC competition, but it was broken in 2022, highlighting the importance of rigorous security analysis.

(The Importance of NIST's Standardization Process):

The National Institute of Standards and Technology (NIST) is playing a crucial role in the transition to PQC. NIST has been running a multi-year standardization process to evaluate and select the most promising PQC algorithms. The goal is to develop a set of standardized PQC algorithms that can be widely adopted and used to secure our data in the quantum age.

(Brief Code Example - Illustrating a Hash Function, a building block for SPHINCS+):

While a complete implementation of a PQC algorithm is too complex for this introductory section, we can illustrate the core concept of a *cryptographic hash function*, which is a fundamental building block for hash-based signatures like SPHINCS+.

```python
import hashlib

def hash_data(data):
  """Hashes the input data using SHA-256."""
  hasher = hashlib.sha256(data.encode('utf-8')) # Ensure
data is encoded as bytes
  return hasher.hexdigest()

# Example usage
data = "This is some data that needs to be hashed."
hashed_data = hash_data(data)
print(f"Original data: {data}")
print(f"Hashed data (SHA-256): {hashed_data}")
```

(Explanation of the Code):

This code uses the hashlib library in Python to hash a string of data using the SHA-256 algorithm. A cryptographic hash function takes an input of any size and produces a fixed-size output (in this case, 256 bits). The key properties of a cryptographic hash function are:

- **One-way:** It's computationally infeasible to reverse the hash function and find the original data from the hash value.
- **Collision-resistant:** It's computationally infeasible to find two different inputs that produce the same hash value.

This code example illustrates the one-way property of hash functions. Even if you know the hash value, it's practically impossible to recover the original data. Hash functions are used in a wide variety of security applications, including password storage, digital signatures, and message authentication. They play a crucial role in PQC, particularly in hash-based signatures.

(*Disclaimer:* This is a very basic example. Real-world cryptographic applications require careful consideration of security best practices and the use of well-vetted cryptographic libraries.)

(The Proactive Nature of PQC):

The key takeaway here is that PQC is a *proactive* defense. We're not waiting for quantum computers to break our cryptography before taking action. We're developing and deploying new cryptographic algorithms *now* to protect our data from future quantum attacks. It's like getting vaccinated against a disease before you're exposed to it.

The transition to PQC will be a complex and challenging process. It will require collaboration between researchers, industry, and government. But it's a necessary step to ensure the security of our digital world in the quantum age. In the following chapters, we'll delve deeper into the different PQC algorithms, explore their strengths and weaknesses, and provide practical guidance on how to implement them in your own systems. So, buckle up, and let's embark on this journey to a quantum-resistant future!

Chapter 2: Quantum Computing Fundamentals for Cybersecurity Professionals

You don't need to become a quantum physicist to grasp the threat that quantum computing poses to cybersecurity. However, understanding some key quantum principles will empower you to make informed decisions about protecting your systems and data. This chapter is your crash course in the essential quantum concepts that every cybersecurity professional should know.

2.1: Qubits, Superposition, and Entanglement: Key Concepts

This is where the rubber meets the road in understanding the power – and threat – of quantum computing. We'll strive for clear explanations, relatable analogies, and a touch of code to solidify these critical concepts.

Think of bits, the foundation of classical computers, like a light switch. It's either on (1) or off (0). Simple, right? Qubits, however, are far more nuanced. A qubit isn't just on or off; it can be *both* on *and* off *at the same time*. This is the mind-bending concept of *superposition*.

(Superposition Explained with Precision): A qubit exists in a probabilistic state, a combination of 0 and 1 until we "look" at it (measure it). Think of it like that spinning coin again. Before it lands, it's neither heads nor tails; it's in a probabilistic state of being both. But the instant it lands, it becomes definitively heads or tails. Similarly, when we measure a qubit, its superposition collapses into either a 0 or a 1.

Mathematically, we represent this state using what's called Dirac notation (or bra-ket notation):

$$|\psi\rangle = \alpha|0\rangle + \beta|1\rangle$$

Let's break that down:

- |ψ⟩: This represents the overall *state* of the qubit. It's the superposition itself.
- |0⟩: This represents the basis state corresponding to the classical bit value "0".
- |1⟩: This represents the basis state corresponding to the classical bit value "1".
- α (alpha) and β (beta): These are *complex numbers* called probability amplitudes. They determine the "weight" or contribution of each basis state to the overall superposition. The square of the magnitude of these amplitudes (i.e., $|\alpha|^2$ and $|\beta|^2$) gives the *probability* of measuring the qubit as 0 or 1, respectively. And because probabilities must add up to 1, we have the crucial condition: $|\alpha|^2 + |\beta|^2 = 1$.

Personal Perspective: The concept of complex numbers being related to probabilities was a major hurdle for me. It's like the universe is speaking in a language that's hardwired differently.

(Code Example: Creating and Visualizing a Superposition):

Let's use Python with the qiskit library (a powerful tool for quantum computing) to create a qubit in superposition and visualize its state. First, you'll need to install qiskit: pip install qiskit qiskit-aer matplotlib

```
import numpy as np
from qiskit import QuantumCircuit, assemble, Aer
from qiskit.visualization import plot_bloch_vector,
plot_histogram
import matplotlib.pyplot as plt

# Define the qubit state: Create a superposition state
# Let's create a superposition where alpha = 1/sqrt(2) and
beta = 1j/sqrt(2)
alpha = 1 / np.sqrt(2)
beta = 1j / np.sqrt(2) # 1j represents the imaginary unit
(sqrt(-1))
initial_state = [alpha, beta]  # Define initial state
vector

# Create a quantum circuit with one qubit
qc = QuantumCircuit(1)

# Initialize the qubit to the specified state
qc.initialize(initial_state, 0)
```

```
# Measure the qubit
qc.measure_all()

# Simulate the circuit using Qiskit's Aer simulator
simulator = Aer.get_backend('qasm_simulator')
compiled_circuit = assemble(qc, simulator)

# Run the simulation 1024 times
job = simulator.run(compiled_circuit, shots=1024)
result = job.result()

# Get the counts (results of measurements)
counts = result.get_counts()

# Display the results
print(f"Measurement results: {counts}")
plot_histogram(counts).show()
plt.show()

# Visualize the qubit on the Bloch sphere.

from qiskit.quantum_info import Statevector
sv = Statevector.from_label('0')
sv = sv.evolve(qc)
plot_bloch_vector(sv).show()
plt.show()
```

(Explanation of the Code):

1. **Import Libraries:** We import necessary libraries from Qiskit and NumPy.
2. **Define the Qubit State:** We define the initial_state vector, which specifies the superposition of the qubit. Here, alpha is 1/sqrt(2) and beta is 1j/sqrt(2). 1j is Python's way of representing the imaginary unit ($\sqrt{-1}$). It creates a superposition that, when measured, results in roughly equal probabilities of 0 and 1.
3. **Create a Quantum Circuit:** We create a quantum circuit with one qubit.
4. **Initialize the Qubit:** We use qc.initialize(initial_state, 0) to set the qubit to our desired superposition.
5. **Measure the Qubit:** We add a measurement to the circuit. This forces the superposition to "collapse" into a definite 0 or 1 state.
6. **Simulate the Circuit:** We use Qiskit's qasm_simulator (a classical simulator) to run the circuit.

7. **Display the Results:** We print the measurement results (the number of times we measured 0 and 1) and plot them using a histogram.
8. **Bloch Sphere Visualization:** The second part of the code visualizes the qubit's state on the Bloch sphere, which is a 3D representation of a qubit's state. This gives you a visual sense of where the qubit lies within its possible superposition states.

(What to Expect in the Output):

You'll see something like this:

```
Measurement results: {'0': 510, '1': 514}
```

The histogram will visually show roughly equal probabilities for measuring 0 and 1. This demonstrates that we successfully created a qubit in superposition.

(Important Note): This is a *simulation* running on a classical computer. It's illustrating how we can *represent* and *manipulate* qubits using classical resources. But to truly harness the power of quantum computing, you need a real quantum computer.

Now, let's talk about *entanglement*, which is often described as "spooky action at a distance."

(Entanglement Demystified): When two or more qubits are entangled, their fates are intertwined. The state of one qubit is correlated with the state of the other, regardless of the distance separating them. If you measure the state of one entangled qubit, you instantly know the state of the other, even if they are light-years apart.

(Relatable Analogy - Revisited): Consider Alice and Bob again. They each have a coin in a box but don't know if it is heads or tails until they open the boxes. Until that point, the coins are in a probabilistic state. Once opened, they are opposite, showing a correlation. That is entanglement.

(Code Example: Creating an Entangled Pair (Bell State)):

Let's create a simple entangled pair of qubits, also known as a Bell state, using Qiskit:

```python
import numpy as np
from qiskit import QuantumCircuit, assemble, Aer
from qiskit.visualization import plot_histogram
import matplotlib.pyplot as plt

# Create a quantum circuit with two qubits and two
classical bits
qc = QuantumCircuit(2, 2)

# Apply a Hadamard gate to the first qubit
qc.h(0)

# Apply a CNOT gate (controlled-NOT) with the first qubit
as control and the second qubit as target
qc.cx(0, 1)

# Measure both qubits
qc.measure([0, 1], [0, 1])

# Simulate the circuit
simulator = Aer.get_backend('qasm_simulator')
compiled_circuit = assemble(qc, simulator)
job = simulator.run(compiled_circuit, shots=1024)
result = job.result()

# Get the counts
counts = result.get_counts()

# Display the results
print(f"Measurement results: {counts}")
plot_histogram(counts).show()
plt.show()
```

(Explanation of the Code):

1. **Create a Quantum Circuit:** We create a quantum circuit with two qubits and two classical bits (to store the measurement results).
2. **Hadamard Gate:** We apply a Hadamard gate to the first qubit, putting it into a superposition.
3. **CNOT Gate:** This is the key to entanglement. The CNOT gate (controlled-NOT) takes two qubits: a control qubit and a target qubit. If the control qubit is in the |1⟩ state, it flips the target qubit. If the control qubit is in the |0⟩ state, it does nothing. By applying a

CNOT gate *after* putting the first qubit into superposition, we create entanglement.

4. **Measure Both Qubits:** We measure both qubits and store the results in the classical bits.
5. **Simulate the Circuit:** We simulate the circuit using Qiskit's qasm_simulator.
6. **Display the Results:** We print the measurement results and plot them using a histogram.

(What to Expect in the Output):

You'll see something like this:

```
Measurement results: {'00': 508, '11': 516}
```

The histogram will show that we only ever measure the states |00⟩ and |11⟩. We *never* see |01⟩ or |10⟩. This is the hallmark of entanglement: the two qubits are perfectly correlated. If we measure the first qubit as 0, we *know* that the second qubit will also be 0. If we measure the first qubit as 1, we *know* that the second qubit will also be 1. They are linked!

Personal Perspective: Even though it's a simulation, seeing that |01⟩ and |10⟩ never show up drives home how tightly coupled these two qubits are.

(Why are Superposition and Entanglement Important?):

Superposition and entanglement are the fundamental building blocks of quantum computing. They allow quantum computers to perform calculations that are impossible for classical computers. Superposition enables massive parallelism, and entanglement enables complex correlations and information sharing. These capabilities are what give quantum computers their potential to break our current cryptographic systems and to solve other complex problems in science and engineering.

(Relating it back to Cybersecurity): Ultimately, understanding qubits, superposition, and entanglement is crucial for cybersecurity professionals because it allows them to:

- Grasp the underlying principles of quantum algorithms like Shor's algorithm.

- Assess the threat that quantum computers pose to their systems and data.
- Evaluate the effectiveness of post-quantum cryptographic solutions.
- Communicate effectively with quantum experts.

While the math and physics behind these concepts can be complex, the fundamental ideas are surprisingly accessible. With a little effort, any cybersecurity professional can gain a solid understanding of qubits, superposition, and entanglement and be well-prepared for the quantum age. Next, we will be discussing about quantum gates and circuits

(2.2: Quantum Gates and Circuits: Building Blocks of Quantum Algorithms)

We're shifting from the theoretical to the more practical side of quantum computing. Just as classical computers are built from logic gates like AND, OR, and NOT, quantum computers are built from *quantum gates*.

Think of quantum gates as the fundamental operations that manipulate qubits. They are the levers and switches that we use to control and transform the quantum state. Unlike classical logic gates, quantum gates must be *reversible*, meaning that they can be undone. This is a consequence of the laws of quantum mechanics.

A quantum gate is mathematically represented by a unitary matrix. A unitary matrix is a complex square matrix whose conjugate transpose is also its inverse. This ensures that the quantum gate preserves the norm of the qubit state, which is a requirement of quantum mechanics.

Let's explore some of the most important quantum gates:

- **Hadamard Gate (H):** We've already encountered the Hadamard gate in the previous section. It's one of the most fundamental quantum gates, and it's used to create superposition. When applied to a qubit in the $|0\rangle$ state, it creates an equal superposition of $|0\rangle$ and $|1\rangle$. The matrix representation of the Hadamard gate is:

$$H = 1/\sqrt{2} \ [\ [1, 1], [1, -1]\ ]$$

- **Pauli-X Gate (X):** The Pauli-X gate is the quantum equivalent of a classical NOT gate. It flips the state of a qubit from |0⟩ to |1⟩ and vice versa. The matrix representation of the Pauli-X gate is:

  X = [[0, 1], [1, 0]]

- **Pauli-Y Gate (Y):** The Pauli-Y gate is another fundamental quantum gate. It performs a rotation around the Y-axis of the Bloch sphere. The matrix representation of the Pauli-Y gate is:

  Y = [[0, -1j], [1j, 0]]

- **Pauli-Z Gate (Z):** The Pauli-Z gate performs a rotation around the Z-axis of the Bloch sphere. The matrix representation of the Pauli-Z gate is:

  Z = [[1, 0], [0, -1]]

- **CNOT Gate (Controlled-NOT):** We also saw the CNOT gate in the previous section. It's a two-qubit gate that performs a controlled-NOT operation. It takes two qubits: a control qubit and a target qubit. If the control qubit is in the |1⟩ state, it flips the target qubit. If the control qubit is in the |0⟩ state, it does nothing. The matrix representation of the CNOT gate is:

  CNOT = [[1, 0, 0, 0], [0, 1, 0, 0], [0, 0, 0, 1], [0, 0, 1, 0]]

Personal Perspective: Thinking of quantum gates as rotations on the Bloch sphere really helped me visualize what they're doing to the qubit.

(Code Example: Building a Quantum Circuit with Multiple Gates):

Let's build a more complex quantum circuit using Qiskit to illustrate how quantum gates are combined to perform a computation:

```
import numpy as np
from qiskit import QuantumCircuit, assemble, Aer
from qiskit.visualization import plot_histogram
import matplotlib.pyplot as plt

# Create a quantum circuit with two qubits and two
classical bits
```

```
qc = QuantumCircuit(2, 2)

# Apply a Hadamard gate to the first qubit
qc.h(0)

# Apply a CNOT gate with the first qubit as control and the
second qubit as target
qc.cx(0, 1)

# Apply a Pauli-X gate to the second qubit
qc.x(1)

# Apply a Hadamard gate to the first qubit again
qc.h(0)

# Measure both qubits
qc.measure([0, 1], [0, 1])

# Simulate the circuit
simulator = Aer.get_backend('qasm_simulator')
compiled_circuit = assemble(qc, simulator)
job = simulator.run(compiled_circuit, shots=1024)
result = job.result()

# Get the counts
counts = result.get_counts()

# Display the results
print(f"Measurement results: {counts}")
plot_histogram(counts).show()
plt.show()
```

(Explanation of the Code):

1. **Create a Quantum Circuit:** We create a quantum circuit with two qubits and two classical bits.
2. **Apply a Hadamard Gate:** We apply a Hadamard gate to the first qubit, putting it into superposition.
3. **Apply a CNOT Gate:** We apply a CNOT gate to entangle the two qubits.
4. **Apply a Pauli-X Gate:** We apply a Pauli-X gate to the second qubit, flipping its state.
5. **Apply a Hadamard Gate Again:** We apply another Hadamard gate to the first qubit.
6. **Measure Both Qubits:** We measure both qubits and store the results in the classical bits.

7. **Simulate the Circuit:** We simulate the circuit using Qiskit's qasm_simulator.
8. **Display the Results:** We print the measurement results and plot them using a histogram.

(What to Expect in the Output):

The output of this code will depend on the specific gates that we apply. It will show the probabilities of measuring the different possible states of the two qubits.

(Quantum Circuits: Orchestrating Quantum Operations):

A *quantum circuit* is a sequence of quantum gates applied to a set of qubits. It's the quantum equivalent of a classical computer program. Designing a quantum algorithm involves carefully constructing a quantum circuit that performs the desired computation. The order of the gates is important and will drastically affect the outcome.

Think of a quantum circuit as a recipe. Each gate is an ingredient, and the order in which you add the ingredients determines the final dish. Similarly, the order in which you apply the quantum gates determines the final state of the qubits.

The quantum gates interact to achieve a given quantum algorithm. This is no different than an orchestra where the instruments contribute different sounds to compose a beautiful musical piece.

Personal Perspective: In order to understand the threat posed by quantum computers, cybersecurity professionals must be familiar with the building blocks of quantum algorithms.

(Relating it back to Shor's Algorithm):

While we can't implement Shor's algorithm in its entirety with the limited resources we have in this book, it's important to understand that Shor's algorithm is built from quantum gates and circuits. It relies on the Quantum Fourier Transform (QFT), which is itself a complex quantum circuit composed of Hadamard gates, controlled-phase gates, and other quantum gates.

The QFT is what gives Shor's algorithm its exponential speedup. It allows the algorithm to efficiently find the period of a periodic function, which is the key to factoring large numbers and solving the discrete logarithm problem.

(Conclusion):

Quantum gates and circuits are the fundamental building blocks of quantum algorithms. By understanding these concepts, cybersecurity professionals can gain a better understanding of the power and potential of quantum computing.

(2.3: Shor's Algorithm: Unveiling the Threat to Public-Key Cryptography)

This is where the rubber meets the road in terms of understanding *why* quantum computing is such a significant concern for cybersecurity. We'll aim for clarity and demystification, focusing on the core principles rather than getting bogged down in complex math.

Shor's algorithm, developed by Peter Shor in 1994, is a quantum algorithm that can factor large numbers exponentially faster than the best-known classical algorithms. This capability is what makes it such a potent threat to our current public-key cryptography, which relies on the difficulty of factoring large numbers. The key is, a quantum computer *efficiently* solves what is *in-efficient* to solve with a classical computer.

(The Core Problem: Factoring Large Numbers):

Let's reiterate why factoring large numbers is so important. Many public-key cryptographic systems, such as RSA, rely on the fact that it's easy to multiply two large prime numbers together, but incredibly difficult to reverse the process – to find the prime factors of the product. This asymmetry is what allows us to create secure encryption keys and digital signatures.

The security of RSA, for example, depends on the assumption that factoring the modulus n (which is the product of two large prime numbers, p and q) is computationally infeasible for classical computers. The larger the numbers, the harder it is to factor them. With current computing power, properly sized keys simply take too long to make factoring feasible.

Personal Perspective: It's like the world's most secure lockbox hinges on the premise that the only way to open it is to try every single combination. But what if a new invention allows you to instantly know the correct combination?

(How Shor's Algorithm Circumvents the Difficulty):

Shor's algorithm circumvents this difficulty by using the principles of quantum mechanics to perform a fundamentally different type of computation. It doesn't just try to factor the number directly; it uses a clever trick involving the *period* of a mathematical function.

The algorithm can be broken down into two main parts:

1. **Quantum Part (Period Finding):** This is where the quantum magic happens. Shor's algorithm uses the Quantum Fourier Transform (QFT) to efficiently find the period of a carefully chosen function.
2. **Classical Part (Post-Processing):** Once the period is found, a classical computer is used to perform some post-processing steps to extract the prime factors.

The real breakthrough is in the *quantum part*. The Quantum Fourier Transform allows the algorithm to explore all possible periods simultaneously, thanks to superposition and entanglement. This is what gives it its exponential speedup.

(A High-Level Overview of the Steps):

Here's a simplified overview of the key steps in Shor's algorithm:

1. **Choose a Random Number:** Choose a random number a that is less than n (the number you want to factor) and relatively prime to n (meaning that a and n have no common factors other than 1).
2. **Find the Period:** Find the period r of the function $f(x) = a^x \bmod n$. The period is the smallest positive integer r such that $a^r \bmod n = 1$. This is where the QFT comes into play. The quantum computer efficiently finds this period r.

3. **Check for Trivial Case:** If r is odd, go back to step 1 and choose a different value of a.
4. **Calculate Factors:** If r is even, calculate the greatest common divisor (GCD) of (a^(r/2) + 1, n) and (a^(r/2) - 1, n). These GCDs are likely to be the prime factors of n.
5. **Verify:** Verify that the calculated factors are indeed the prime factors of n.

(Why the Quantum Fourier Transform (QFT) is Key):

The Quantum Fourier Transform (QFT) is a quantum algorithm that performs a discrete Fourier transform on a quantum state. It's the quantum equivalent of the Fast Fourier Transform (FFT), which is a widely used algorithm in classical signal processing.

The QFT allows Shor's algorithm to efficiently find the period of the function f(x) = a^x mod n. Without the QFT, finding the period would be a computationally intractable problem for classical computers. But with the QFT, it becomes a manageable task for a quantum computer.

The QFT leverages superposition and entanglement to explore all possible periods simultaneously. It essentially performs a massive parallel search, allowing it to find the period much faster than any classical algorithm.

Personal Perspective: The QFT is like a magical magnifying glass that allows us to zoom in on the hidden patterns and periodicities in the data. It's a beautiful example of how quantum mechanics can be used to solve problems that are intractable for classical computers.

(Code Illustration: The Classical Part of Shor's Algorithm):

While we can't implement the full quantum part of Shor's algorithm with readily available code, we can illustrate the *classical* post-processing steps. This code assumes that we have already obtained the period r from the quantum part of the algorithm. This will help solidify what happens *after* a quantum computer performs its calculations.

```
import math

def gcd(a, b):
    """Calculates the greatest common divisor (GCD) of two
numbers."""
```

```python
    while b:
        a, b = b, a % b
    return a

def shors_classical(n, a, r):
  """Performs the classical post-processing steps of Shor's
algorithm.

  Args:
    n: The number to factorize.
    a: A random number relatively prime to n.
    r: The period found by the quantum part of Shor's
algorithm.

  Returns:
    A tuple containing the two factors, or None if
factorization fails.
    """

  if r % 2 != 0:
    print("Period is odd. Factorization fails.")
    return None, None

  x = pow(a, r // 2, n)   # Calculate a^(r/2) mod n

  if x == -1 % n:
    print("x == -1 mod n. Factorization fails.")
    return None, None

  factor1 = gcd(x + 1, n)
  factor2 = gcd(x - 1, n)

  if factor1 == 1 or factor2 == 1 or factor1 == n or
factor2 == n:
      print("Trivial factors found. Factorization fails.")
      return None, None

  print(f"Found factors: {factor1}, {factor2}")
  return factor1, factor2

# Example Usage (assuming we know the period r)
n = 15   # The number to factorize
a = 7    # A random number relatively prime to n
r = 4    # Assume the quantum part found the period to be 4

factor1, factor2 = shors_classical(n, a, r)

if factor1 and factor2:
    print(f"The factors of {n} are: {factor1} and
{factor2}")
```

(Explanation of the Code):

1. **gcd(a, b) Function:** This function calculates the greatest common divisor (GCD) of two numbers using Euclid's algorithm.
2. **shors_classical(n, a, r) Function:** This function implements the classical post-processing steps of Shor's algorithm.
   - It first checks if the period r is even. If it's odd, the factorization fails.
   - It then calculates $x = a^{(r/2)} \bmod n$.
   - It calculates the GCD of $(x + 1, n)$ and $(x - 1, n)$. These GCDs are likely to be the prime factors of n.
   - It returns the two factors.
3. **Example Usage:** The code demonstrates how to use the shors_classical function to factorize the number 15, assuming that we know the period r to be 4.

(Important Note): This code is only the *classical* part of Shor's algorithm. It assumes that we have already obtained the period r from the quantum part of the algorithm. This code cannot factor large numbers on its own.

(The Impact on Public-Key Cryptography - Re-emphasized):

With all this in mind, let's bring it all together. What does Shor's algorithm actually *do* to our cryptography?

1. **RSA is Rendered Useless:** A quantum computer running Shor's algorithm can efficiently factor the large numbers used in RSA encryption, allowing it to decrypt RSA-encrypted messages and forge digital signatures.
2. **ECC is Compromised:** Similarly, a quantum computer can efficiently solve the discrete logarithm problem on elliptic curves, breaking ECC encryption and compromising key exchange protocols.
3. **Diffie-Hellman Falls:** The same fate awaits Diffie-Hellman key exchange, as it's also vulnerable to Shor's algorithm.

This is a *fundamental* problem. It's not just a matter of using longer keys or tweaking the algorithms. The underlying mathematical principles that our cryptography relies on are simply no longer secure in the face of quantum computers.

Shor's algorithm represents a profound threat to our current public-key cryptography. By efficiently factoring large numbers and solving the discrete logarithm problem, it undermines the security of RSA, ECC, and Diffie-Hellman. While we can't fully implement Shor's algorithm with readily available code, understanding its core principles is crucial for appreciating the urgency of the quantum threat and the importance of transitioning to post-quantum cryptography.

(2.4: The Current State of Quantum Computer Development and Timelines)

As we've established, the theoretical threat posed by Shor's algorithm is significant. But theory alone doesn't break encryption. *Actual* quantum computers need to be built and scaled to the point where they can execute Shor's algorithm on the key sizes used in real-world cryptographic systems. That's a very tall order.

(Key Metrics for Quantum Computer Development):

It's not just about the number of qubits. Several key metrics determine the power and usefulness of a quantum computer:

- **Qubit Count:** The number of qubits is a necessary but not sufficient condition for building a useful quantum computer. You need enough qubits to represent the problem you're trying to solve. For breaking RSA, thousands of *stable, high-quality* qubits will be required.
- **Coherence Time:** Qubits are fragile. They easily lose their quantum properties (superposition and entanglement) due to interactions with the environment. This loss of quantum information is called decoherence. The longer a qubit can maintain its coherence, the more complex computations it can perform.
- **Gate Fidelity (Accuracy):** Quantum gates are not perfect. They introduce errors into the computation. The higher the gate fidelity, the more accurate the computation.
- **Connectivity:** Connectivity refers to how easily qubits can interact with each other. In some quantum computer architectures, qubits

can only interact with their nearest neighbors. This limits the types of algorithms that can be implemented.
- **Scalability:** Scalability refers to how easily the number of qubits can be increased. Building a quantum computer with thousands or millions of qubits is a significant engineering challenge.
- **Error Correction:** Quantum computers are inherently noisy, and quantum error correction is essential to mitigate the effects of noise. Quantum error correction requires even *more* qubits, adding to the overall resource requirements.

Personal Perspective: It's often said that building a quantum computer is like building a house of cards on top of a washing machine. You're trying to maintain delicate quantum states in the face of constant noise and vibrations.

(Different Quantum Computing Technologies):

There are several different technologies being used to build quantum computers:

- **Superconducting Qubits:** This is the most mature technology. Companies like IBM, Google, and Rigetti are using superconducting qubits. Superconducting qubits are based on the phenomenon of superconductivity, where certain materials lose all resistance to electrical current at very low temperatures. These qubits are fabricated using techniques similar to those used to make classical microchips.
- **Trapped Ion Qubits:** This technology uses individual ions (electrically charged atoms) that are trapped and controlled using electromagnetic fields. Companies like IonQ are using trapped ion qubits. Trapped ion qubits have very long coherence times and high gate fidelities, but they are more difficult to scale up than superconducting qubits.
- **Photonic Qubits:** This technology uses photons (particles of light) as qubits. Photonic qubits have the advantage of being less susceptible to noise than other types of qubits, but they are also more difficult to control and manipulate.
- **Neutral Atom Qubits:** This technology uses neutral atoms (atoms with no net charge) as qubits. Neutral atom qubits are similar to trapped ion qubits, but they are easier to scale up.

- **Other Technologies:** There are also other quantum computing technologies being explored, such as topological qubits and silicon qubits.

Each technology has its own strengths and weaknesses. There is no clear winner at this point. The best technology for building a quantum computer may depend on the specific application.

(Current State of Quantum Computer Development):

Currently, quantum computers are still in the early stages of development. They are not yet powerful enough to break our current cryptography. The largest quantum computers have only a few hundred qubits, and those qubits are still relatively noisy. The road to thousands of stable, high-quality qubits is still years off.

However, significant progress is being made. Companies like IBM, Google, and Rigetti are regularly releasing new quantum processors with more qubits and improved performance. Researchers are also making progress in developing quantum error correction techniques.

Personal Perspective: I think we're at a point similar to where classical computing was in the 1950s. We have the basic building blocks, but we're still figuring out how to put them together to build truly useful computers.

(Timelines for Building a Cryptographically Relevant Quantum Computer (CRQC)):

Predicting the future is always difficult, but most experts believe that a CRQC is still several years away. There is considerable debate and uncertainty.

Some factors that will influence the timeline:

- **Sustained Investment:** Continued funding and research are critical.
- **Breakthroughs in Qubit Technology:** Progress in qubit coherence, gate fidelity, and scalability is essential.
- **Advances in Quantum Error Correction:** Practical quantum error correction is a must.

- **Algorithm Optimization:** More efficient quantum algorithms could lower the qubit requirements.

Here are some general timeline estimates, keeping in mind they are highly speculative:

- **Near-Term (5-10 years):** Expect continued progress in qubit count and performance, but still not enough to break RSA. Quantum computers may be useful for solving some niche problems in materials science and drug discovery.
- **Mid-Term (10-20 years):** A CRQC is possible, but not guaranteed. Significant breakthroughs in qubit technology and error correction will be needed.
- **Long-Term (20+ years):** A CRQC is more likely, but still uncertain. The exact timeline will depend on the pace of technological innovation.

(The "Harvest Now, Decrypt Later" Threat - Revisited Again):

Even if a CRQC is still years away, the "harvest now, decrypt later" threat is real. Adversaries could be collecting encrypted data today, storing it, and waiting for quantum computers to become powerful enough to decrypt it. This is especially concerning for data that needs to remain confidential for many years.

(What Should Cybersecurity Professionals Do?):

- **Stay Informed:** Keep up-to-date on the latest developments in quantum computing and PQC.
- **Assess Your Risks:** Evaluate the potential impact of quantum computers on your organization's data and systems.
- **Plan for Migration:** Develop a plan for migrating to PQC algorithms.
- **Engage with Experts:** Consult with cryptography experts and quantum computing researchers.
- **Advocate for Standards:** Support the development and adoption of PQC standards.

(Can we provide code examples to illustrate this section? No.) The current level of quantum computer development is far below running any of the real-world encryption algorithms. So, no. But it does give us an opportunity to restate that as we are talking about this subject, that the situation continues to rapidly evolve and to stay up to date.

(Conclusion):

The timeline for building a cryptographically relevant quantum computer is uncertain, but the threat is real. Cybersecurity professionals need to stay informed, assess their risks, plan for migration to PQC, and engage with experts. The quantum age is coming, and we need to be prepared.

Chapter 3: "The Race to Quantum-Safe Standards: NIST's PQC Standardization Process

This chapter is about the crucial work being done to ensure we have reliable, interoperable, and secure defenses against quantum attacks. We'll explore the motivations, the process, and the players involved in this global effort.

Imagine you're building a bridge. You wouldn't just use any old materials and construction techniques, right? You'd rely on established engineering standards to ensure the bridge is safe, durable, and can handle the expected load. The same principle applies to cryptography. We need well-defined standards to ensure that our PQC algorithms are secure, efficient, and can be widely adopted.

(3.1: The Urgent Need for Post-Quantum Standards):

Imagine a world where every country, every company, and every individual used their own unique language to communicate. It would be chaotic, inefficient, and prone to misunderstandings. The same principle applies to cryptography. If everyone used different, non-standardized PQC algorithms, the resulting chaos would be a cybersecurity nightmare.

(The Chaos of a Non-Standardized World):

Without PQC standards, we'd face a number of serious problems:

- **Interoperability Issues:** Different systems and applications would be unable to communicate securely with each other. Sending an encrypted message from one system to another would be like trying to translate a message from one obscure language to another without a dictionary.
- **Increased Complexity:** Developers would have to support multiple PQC algorithms, increasing the complexity and cost of software development.

- **Security Risks:** Non-standardized algorithms are more likely to have security vulnerabilities. Without rigorous peer review and analysis, it's difficult to ensure that an algorithm is truly secure.
- **Vendor Lock-in:** Companies might be forced to rely on proprietary PQC algorithms from specific vendors, limiting their choices and increasing their costs.
- **Lack of Trust:** Users would have little confidence in the security of non-standardized algorithms. Without a trusted standard, it's difficult to know which algorithms are truly secure.

Personal Perspective: I've seen firsthand the problems that arise when systems don't adhere to open standards. It creates a fragmented ecosystem where everything is more difficult and less secure.

The urgency of PQC standards stems from two key factors:

1. **The Quantum Threat is Real:** While a cryptographically relevant quantum computer (CRQC) is not yet a reality, the threat is real and growing. As quantum computers continue to develop, the risk of a quantum attack on our cryptographic infrastructure increases.
2. **Migration Takes Time:** Migrating to PQC algorithms is a complex and time-consuming process. It requires careful planning, testing, and deployment. If we wait until a CRQC is built before starting the migration, it will be too late. The "harvest now, decrypt later" threat means that our data is at risk *today*.

(Why Proactive Standardization is Essential):

Proactive standardization is essential to ensure that we have secure and interoperable PQC algorithms ready to go when they are needed. By developing standards *before* the quantum threat becomes a reality, we can:

- **Reduce the Risk of a Quantum Attack:** Having standardized PQC algorithms in place will make it more difficult for attackers to exploit the quantum threat.
- **Ensure Interoperability:** Standardized algorithms will allow different systems and applications to communicate securely with each other.
- **Reduce Complexity:** Standardized algorithms will simplify software development and reduce costs.

- **Build Trust:** Standardized algorithms will give users confidence in the security of their systems and data.

(Relatable Analogy): Think of it like building a fire escape. You don't wait until the building is on fire before building the fire escape. You build it beforehand, so that people can escape safely in the event of a fire. Similarly, we need to develop PQC standards now, so that we can migrate to quantum-resistant cryptography before the quantum threat becomes a reality.

It is critical to point out the proactive nature of the situation at hand. Unlike responding to a threat with reactive patching of security software, PQC requires proactive measures before the actual threat becomes realized in quantum computers.

(Code Illustration: While it's hard to directly demonstrate standardization, we can illustrate how standardized hashing algorithms are used in broader security contexts. This reinforces the idea of relying on known, reliable algorithms):

```python
import hashlib

def secure_password_hash(password, salt):
    """Hashes a password using a standardized algorithm
(SHA-256) with a salt.

    Args:
        password: The password to hash (string).
        salt: A random salt to add to the password
(string).

    Returns:
        The hexadecimal representation of the salted
password hash (string).
    """

    # Combine the password and salt
    salted_password = salt + password
    salted_password_bytes = salted_password.encode('utf-8')
# Encode to bytes

    # Hash the salted password using SHA-256
    hashed_password =
hashlib.sha256(salted_password_bytes).hexdigest()

    return hashed_password
```

```
# Example Usage
password = "mysecretpassword"
salt = "randomsalt123" # In practice, generate a
cryptographically secure random salt

hashed_password = secure_password_hash(password, salt)

print(f"Password: {password}")
print(f"Salt: {salt}")
print(f"Hashed Password (SHA-256): {hashed_password}")
```

(Explanation of the Code):

1. **Import hashlib:** Imports the hashlib library for hashing algorithms.
2. **secure_password_hash Function:**
    o Takes the password and a salt as input.
    o Combines the salt and password to prevent rainbow table attacks.
    o Encodes the combined string to bytes using UTF-8, which is required for the hashlib functions.
    o Hashes the salted_password_bytes using the SHA-256 algorithm.
    o Returns the hexadecimal representation of the hash using .hexdigest().
3. **Example Usage:**
    o Sets a sample password and salt. **Important:** In real-world applications, the salt should be generated using a cryptographically secure random number generator, and it should be unique for each password.
    o Calls the secure_password_hash function to hash the password with the salt.
    o Prints the original password, salt, and the resulting hashed_password.

(Key Takeaway): The hashlib library provides access to standardized hashing algorithms like SHA-256. Using these standardized algorithms ensures that your password hashes are secure and interoperable. Without standardization, every developer might invent their own hashing algorithm, leading to a chaotic and insecure landscape. This is what we want to *avoid* with PQC.

(The Risk of Delay - Re-Emphasized):

Delaying the development and deployment of PQC standards would have serious consequences:

- **Increased Vulnerability:** Our systems would remain vulnerable to quantum attacks for longer.
- **Higher Migration Costs:** Migrating to PQC algorithms would be more expensive and complex if we wait until the last minute.
- **Loss of Trust:** Users would lose trust in the security of our systems and data.

The time to act is now. We need to support the development and adoption of PQC standards to ensure that our digital world remains secure in the quantum age.

(3.2: NIST's PQC Competition: Goals, Criteria, and Evaluation Process):

To secure cryptographic algorithms against a variety of threats, the National Institute of Standards and Technology (NIST) initiated a formal public competition to solicit candidate algorithms. After a thorough multi-year evaluation process, NIST planned to select a small number of these algorithms for standardization.

Think of the NIST PQC competition as the Olympics of cryptography. Instead of athletes competing for medals, cryptographers from around the world competed to have their algorithms chosen as the new global standards for PQC. The competition was open to anyone, and the submissions were publicly available. It's about a global community collaborating to find robust solutions.

(The Goals of the NIST PQC Competition):

The overarching goals of the NIST PQC competition were multifaceted, aimed at both immediate security and long-term cryptographic health. The primary objectives were:

- **Identify Secure and Efficient PQC Algorithms:** The core goal was to find algorithms resistant to attacks from both classical and quantum computers. Crucially, these algorithms needed to perform efficiently enough for use in real-world applications. It wasn't just about theoretical security; practicality was paramount.

- **Establish Open Standards:** NIST aimed to create open, royalty-free standards that anyone could implement and use. This was crucial for ensuring interoperability and preventing vendor lock-in. The goal was to create a level playing field where everyone could benefit from PQC.
- **Promote Innovation and Research:** The competition was designed to stimulate research and development in the field of PQC. By providing a clear set of goals and criteria, NIST encouraged cryptographers to develop new and innovative algorithms.
- **Increase Public Confidence:** The transparent and rigorous evaluation process was intended to build public confidence in the selected PQC algorithms.

Personal Perspective: What impressed me most about the NIST competition was its commitment to transparency. Every submission, every evaluation, every comment was publicly available. This allowed anyone to follow the process and contribute to the analysis of the algorithms. It truly was a global effort.

(The Criteria for Evaluation):

Submitting an algorithm to NIST was one thing. Successfully navigating the competition required meeting a stringent set of requirements across multiple categories. NIST employed a range of criteria to evaluate submitted algorithms:

- **Security (Primary):** This was the paramount consideration. NIST sought assurance that the algorithms could withstand the most sophisticated attacks, both now and in the foreseeable future. This involved theoretical analysis of the algorithm's mathematical foundations, as well as practical testing to identify potential weaknesses. Security was graded first and foremost.
- **Performance (Secondary but Crucial):** Security alone was not enough. The algorithms needed to be efficient in terms of computational resources, memory usage, and bandwidth. The algorithm should not come at too high of a cost relative to performance.

- **Implementation Characteristics:** NIST considered how easily the algorithms could be implemented in both hardware and software. Factors such as code size, memory footprint, and power consumption were taken into account. An algorithm might be secure but not worth the practical tradeoff.
- **Intellectual Property Considerations:** NIST aimed to select algorithms with clear and unencumbered intellectual property rights. Algorithms with complex licensing requirements or patent restrictions were disfavored. NIST looked for freedom of use for developers around the globe.
- **Algorithm and Implementation Maturity:** Longer-standing code that has been tested will rank higher than relatively new code that has not been widely used and tested.

(The Multi-Round Evaluation Process):

The NIST PQC competition was structured as a multi-round process, allowing algorithms to mature and be thoroughly vetted over time. This involved:

1. **Call for Submissions:** NIST issued a public call for submissions, inviting cryptographers from around the world to submit their PQC algorithms.
2. **Initial Review:** NIST conducted an initial review of the submissions to ensure that they met the basic requirements for security and performance.
3. **Public Evaluation:** The submissions were made publicly available, and experts from around the world were invited to analyze the algorithms and submit comments and criticisms.
4. **NIST Evaluation:** NIST conducted its own independent evaluation of the algorithms, using a variety of techniques, including cryptanalysis, performance testing, and implementation analysis.
5. **Round-Based Progression:** Based on the results of the public and NIST evaluations, the algorithms were advanced to subsequent rounds. Algorithms that were found to have significant weaknesses were eliminated from the competition.
6. **Final Selection:** After several rounds of evaluation, NIST selected a small number of algorithms for standardization.

Personal Perspective: The back-and-forth between the submitters and the evaluators was fascinating to watch. It was a real-time example of how the scientific method works, with hypotheses being tested, challenged, and refined.

(The Transparent Nature of the Competition):

The NIST PQC competition was notable for its transparency. All the submissions, evaluations, and comments were publicly available on the NIST website. This allowed anyone to follow the process, contribute to the analysis of the algorithms, and understand the reasons behind NIST's decisions. Transparency builds public trust and encourages wider adoption.

(The Winners and the Future):

In 2022, NIST announced the initial set of algorithms to be standardized: CRYSTALS-Kyber, CRYSTALS-Dilithium, SPHINCS+, and Classic McEliece. These algorithms represent a significant step forward in securing our digital infrastructure against quantum attacks.

The NIST PQC competition is an ongoing process. NIST is continuing to evaluate other candidate algorithms for potential standardization in future rounds. The threat landscape is constantly evolving, and it's important to have a pipeline of new and innovative algorithms to stay ahead of the curve.

(Practical Code Example Demonstrating Algorithm Performance - SHA3 vs. SHA2):

Let's demonstrate the performance of SHA-3 (one of the underlying components for some selected NIST algorithms) versus SHA-2 hashing algorithms to understand the concept of performance evaluation. Note that while not directly a PQC algorithm, it helps to understand performance tradeoffs.

```
    import hashlib
import time

def hash_performance(algorithm, data):
    """Measures the performance of a hashing algorithm.
```

```
    Args:
        algorithm: The hashlib algorithm to use (e.g.,
hashlib.sha256).
        data: The data to hash (bytes).

    Returns:
        The time taken to hash the data in seconds.
    """
    start_time = time.time()
    algorithm(data).hexdigest()
    end_time = time.time()
    return end_time - start_time

# Data to hash (let's use a 1MB file as an example)
data_size = 1024 * 1024  # 1MB
data = b"This is some example data." * (data_size //
len(b"This is some example data."))

# Measure the performance of SHA-256
sha256_time = hash_performance(hashlib.sha256, data)

# Measure the performance of SHA3-256
sha3_256_time = hash_performance(hashlib.sha3_256, data)

print(f"SHA-256 hashing time: {sha256_time:.4f} seconds")
print(f"SHA3-256 hashing time: {sha3_256_time:.4f}
seconds")
```

(Explanation of the Code):

- **hash_performance Function:** This function measures the time taken to hash a given amount of data using a specified hashing algorithm. It takes the algorithm (e.g., hashlib.sha256) and the data as input, hashes the data, and returns the elapsed time.
- **Data Creation:** We create a 1MB chunk of data to hash, ensuring that we test the hashing algorithms with a reasonable amount of data.
- **Performance Measurement:** We call the hash_performance function for both SHA-256 and SHA3-256, and we print the results.

When you run this code, you'll likely see that SHA-256 is faster than SHA3-256. This is because SHA-256 is a more mature algorithm with highly optimized implementations. SHA3-256, while providing stronger security guarantees, is generally slower.

The final code is a *simulation*. This example emphasizes the type of test for choosing the type of code to run for PQC.

The purpose of PQC competition, is to create a global algorithm that can be widely accepted across the world. This can be achieved through open dialogue, testing, and assessment.

(3.3: Overview of PQC Algorithm Families):

We're moving past the general need and process for PQC; now it's time to start exploring the solutions. Different underlying mathematical structures can create secure code. These include lattice, code, hash, multivariate, and isogeny based algorithms. Each come with their respective strengths and weaknesses.

(Lattice-Based Cryptography: Math in High Dimensions):

Imagine arranging points in a regular, repeating pattern in multi-dimensional space. This is the basic idea of a *lattice*. Lattice-based cryptography relies on the difficulty of solving certain problems on these lattices.

Specifically, lattice-based schemes often leverage the *Learning With Errors (LWE)* problem and its more efficient variant, *Module Learning With Errors (MLWE)*. In essence, you're given a set of linear equations with some added noise (the "errors"). The goal is to find the secret values that satisfy the equations, even with the errors.

(Why is this hard?): As the dimensionality of the lattice increases and the amount of noise increases, the problem becomes exponentially harder for both classical and quantum computers.

(Key Advantages of Lattice-Based Cryptography):

- **Strong Security Foundations:** Lattice problems have been studied for decades, and there's a growing body of evidence suggesting that they are indeed hard to solve, even with quantum computers.
- **Good Performance:** Lattice-based algorithms generally offer good performance, making them suitable for a wide range of

applications. They provide relatively fast key generation, encryption, decryption, and signature generation.
- **Versatility:** Lattice-based cryptography can be used to construct both encryption schemes and digital signature algorithms.

(Example PQC Algorithms: CRYSTALS-Kyber (key exchange) and CRYSTALS-Dilithium (digital signatures) are prominent examples, both selected by NIST for standardization.

(Code Example - Simplified Illustration of Lattice Reduction Concept):

While implementing full lattice-based cryptography is beyond the scope of a single example, we can illustrate the basic idea of *lattice reduction*. Lattice reduction is a technique used to find shorter, more convenient vectors in a lattice.

```python
import numpy as np

def generate_lattice(basis_vectors):
  """Generates a set of lattice points based on the given
basis vectors."""
  lattice_points = []
  for i in range(-2, 3):  # Iterate over a small range of
integers
    for j in range(-2, 3):
      point = i * basis_vectors[0] + j * basis_vectors[1]
      lattice_points.append(point)
  return lattice_points

def visualize_lattice(lattice_points):
  """Visualizes the lattice points using matplotlib."""
  import matplotlib.pyplot as plt
  x = [point[0] for point in lattice_points]
  y = [point[1] for point in lattice_points]
  plt.scatter(x, y)
  plt.xlabel("X")
  plt.ylabel("Y")
  plt.title("Lattice Points")
  plt.grid(True)
  plt.show()

# Define two basis vectors (example)
basis_vectors = [np.array([2, 1]), np.array([1, 3])]

# Generate lattice points
lattice_points = generate_lattice(basis_vectors)
```

```
# Visualize the lattice
visualize_lattice(lattice_points)
```

(Explanation of the Code):

1. **generate_lattice(basis_vectors) Function:** This function takes a list of basis vectors as input and generates a set of lattice points by taking linear combinations of the basis vectors.
2. **visualize_lattice(lattice_points) Function:** This function takes a list of lattice points as input and visualizes them using matplotlib.
3. **Basis Vector Definition:** We define two basis vectors ([2, 1] and [1, 3]).
4. **Lattice Generation and Visualization:** The code generates a set of lattice points and visualizes them.

By looking at the plotted lattice, imagine trying to find the "shortest" vector that leads to a specific point. It's not always obvious, especially in higher dimensions with added noise. This difficulty is the foundation of lattice-based cryptography.

(Important Disclaimer): This is a *very* simplified illustration. Real lattice reduction algorithms are far more complex and operate in much higher dimensions.

(Code-Based Cryptography: Error Correction as Security):

Imagine sending a message across a noisy channel. Some of the bits might get flipped along the way. Error-correcting codes allow you to detect and correct these errors, ensuring that the message arrives intact. Code-based cryptography turns this idea on its head, using the difficulty of decoding *random* linear codes as the basis for security.

The most prominent example is *Classic McEliece*, which is based on the McEliece cryptosystem from 1978. McEliece uses Goppa codes, a special type of linear code with efficient decoding algorithms. The public key is a disguised version of the Goppa code, and the private key is the original Goppa code. Encryption involves adding errors to the message, and decryption involves using the private key to correct the errors.

(Why is this hard?): While decoding Goppa codes is easy with the private key, decoding a *random* linear code is believed to be a very difficult problem, even for quantum computers.

(Key Advantages of Code-Based Cryptography):

- **Long History:** The McEliece cryptosystem has been around for over 40 years and has withstood extensive cryptanalysis.
- **Different Mathematical Structure:** Code-based cryptography is based on a completely different mathematical problem than lattice-based cryptography. This provides diversification, reducing the risk that a breakthrough in one area will break all PQC algorithms.

(Notable Trade-offs):

- **Large Key Sizes:** Code-based cryptography typically has larger key sizes than other PQC algorithms, which can be a concern for some applications.

(Hash-Based Signatures: Simplicity and Provable Security):

Hash-based signatures are based on the security properties of cryptographic hash functions. A cryptographic hash function takes an input of any size and produces a fixed-size output (the hash value). The hash function should be one-way (difficult to reverse) and collision-resistant (difficult to find two different inputs that produce the same hash value).

Hash-based signatures are built using Merkle trees. A Merkle tree is a binary tree where each node contains the hash of its children. The leaves of the tree contain the hashes of the messages that are being signed.

(How it works): To sign a message, the signer computes the hash of the message and then reveals a portion of the Merkle tree that allows the verifier to verify that the hash of the message is indeed a leaf in the Merkle tree.

(Why is this hard?): The security of hash-based signatures relies on the security of the underlying hash function. If the hash function is one-way and collision-resistant, then it's difficult to forge a signature.

(Key Advantages of Hash-Based Signatures):

- **Simplicity:** Hash-based signatures are relatively simple to implement and understand.
- **Provable Security:** The security of hash-based signatures can be mathematically proven based on the security of the underlying hash function.
- **Resistance to Quantum Attacks:** Hash-based signatures are believed to be resistant to attacks from quantum computers.

(Key Drawbacks):

- **State Management (for some schemes):** Some hash-based signature schemes require careful state management, which can be complex to implement securely.
- **Signature Size:** Signatures can be relatively large.

(Example PQC Algorithms: SPHINCS+ is a stateless hash-based signature scheme selected by NIST for standardization.

(Brief mention of Multivariate and Isogeny-Based - with Caveats):

- **Multivariate Cryptography:** Relies on solving systems of polynomial equations. While promising, it has faced challenges in finding parameters that provide strong security and practical performance.
- **Isogeny-Based Cryptography:** Relies on the difficulty of finding isogenies between elliptic curves. It had attractive properties like small key sizes, but the breaking of SIKE underscored the need for caution.

Personal Perspective: The diversity of these PQC approaches is what gives me confidence in the long-term security of our cryptographic infrastructure. If one approach turns out to be flawed, we have others to fall back on.

(Conclusion):

The world of PQC is rich and diverse, with a variety of algorithms offering different approaches to resisting quantum attacks. Each family has its own strengths and weaknesses, and the choice of which algorithm to use will depend on the specific application and the security requirements. Having this diversity, and carefully vetting each type of code is what creates a secure future.

(3.4: The Importance of Open Standards and Public Scrutiny):

Imagine a city building its infrastructure – roads, bridges, utilities – in complete secrecy. No public input, no expert review, just a small group making all the decisions behind closed doors. The result would likely be a poorly designed, inefficient, and potentially dangerous system. The same is true for cryptography. Secrecy breeds weakness, while openness fosters strength.

(Open Standards: A Foundation for Interoperability and Innovation):

Open standards are publicly available specifications for cryptographic algorithms and protocols. Anyone can implement these standards without paying royalties or licensing fees. This is crucial for ensuring interoperability, reducing complexity, and promoting innovation.

(Why are open standards so important?):

- **Interoperability:** Open standards allow different systems and applications to communicate securely with each other. This is essential for a global internet where devices and services from different vendors need to work together seamlessly.
- **Reduced Complexity:** Open standards simplify software development by providing a common set of building blocks. Developers don't have to reinvent the wheel every time they need to implement cryptography.
- **Increased Competition:** Open standards promote competition by allowing multiple vendors to offer implementations of the same algorithms. This drives down costs and increases innovation.
- **Long-Term Viability:** Open standards are more likely to be maintained and supported over the long term. Because they are not tied to a single vendor, they are less likely to become obsolete or abandoned.
- **Wider Adoption:** Openness makes the code more accessible, leading to broader usage.

Personal Perspective: I've always been a strong advocate for open source and open standards. I believe that they are essential for building a more secure and equitable digital world.

(Public Scrutiny: The Power of Collective Intelligence):

Public scrutiny is the process of subjecting cryptographic algorithms and protocols to intense review and analysis by experts from around the world. This involves:

- **Publishing the Algorithm:** Making the full specification of the algorithm publicly available.
- **Inviting Feedback:** Actively soliciting comments, criticisms, and proposed attacks from cryptographers and security researchers.
- **Responding to Feedback:** Addressing any issues that are identified and incorporating improvements into the algorithm.
- **Open Source Implementations:** Releasing open source code.

(Why is public Security so important?):

- **Increased Security:** Public scrutiny helps to identify and eliminate security vulnerabilities. The more eyes that are looking at an algorithm, the more likely it is that any weaknesses will be found.
- **Improved Design:** Public scrutiny can lead to improvements in the design of an algorithm. By incorporating feedback from experts, the algorithm can be made more efficient, more robust, and easier to implement.
- **Increased Confidence:** Public scrutiny builds confidence in the security of an algorithm. If an algorithm has been subjected to intense review and has withstood all known attacks, users are more likely to trust it.
- **Diverse Perspectives:** Public scrutiny brings together diverse perspectives and expertise. Researchers from different backgrounds and with different areas of specialization can contribute to the analysis of the algorithm.

(Relatable Analogy): Think of it like a peer-reviewed scientific paper. Before a scientific paper is published, it is subjected to intense review by other experts in the field. This helps to ensure that the research is sound and that the conclusions are valid. Cryptographic algorithms need the same kind of rigorous peer review.

(The NIST PQC Competition as a Model for Openness and Scrutiny):

The NIST PQC competition is a prime example of how open standards and public scrutiny can lead to better cryptography. The entire process was conducted in a transparent and open manner. All the submissions, evaluations, and comments were publicly available on the NIST website. This allowed anyone to follow the process, contribute to the analysis of the algorithms, and understand the reasons behind NIST's decisions. This model is an example to the world.

(Code Example: Illustrating the Importance of Using Well-Vetted Cryptographic Libraries):

While we can't directly demonstrate the process of public scrutiny with code, we can illustrate the importance of using well-vetted and widely used cryptographic libraries. These libraries have been subjected to extensive review and testing, increasing confidence in their security.

```python
from cryptography.hazmat.primitives import hashes
from cryptography.hazmat.backends import default_backend

def hash_data(data):
    """Hashes the input data using SHA-256 from the
cryptography library.

    Args:
        data: The data to hash (bytes).

    Returns:
        The hexadecimal representation of the hash
(string).
    """
    digest = hashes.Hash(hashes.SHA256(),
backend=default_backend())
    digest.update(data)
    return digest.finalize().hex()

# Example Usage
data = b"This is some sensitive data."
hashed_data = hash_data(data)

print(f"Original data: {data.decode()}")
print(f"Hashed data (SHA-256): {hashed_data}")
```

(Explanation of the Code):

55

1. **Import Necessary Modules:** We import the hashes module from the cryptography.hazmat.primitives package and the default_backend from cryptography.hazmat.backends.
2. **hash_data Function:**
   o Takes the data to hash (as bytes) as input.
   o Creates a Hash object, specifying the SHA-256 algorithm and the backend to use.
   o Updates the Hash object with the data to be hashed.
   o Finalizes the hash calculation and returns the hexadecimal representation of the hash.
3. **Example Usage:**
   o Sets the data to be hashed.
   o Calls the hash_data function to hash the data.
   o Prints the original data and the resulting hashed_data.

(Key Takeaway): The cryptography library is a widely used and well-vetted cryptographic library for Python. By using this library, you can be confident that the SHA-256 implementation is secure and reliable. Avoid implementing your own cryptographic algorithms unless you are a cryptography expert. The cryptography.io library is well tested and provides secure tools for cryptography.

(The Consequences of Closed-Source Cryptography):

Closed-source cryptography, where the algorithm and implementation are kept secret, is generally considered to be a bad idea. Without public scrutiny, it's impossible to know whether the algorithm is truly secure. There have been numerous examples of closed-source cryptographic systems that have been broken, often with devastating consequences.

(Conclusion):

Open standards and public scrutiny are essential for building trust in cryptographic algorithms. The NIST PQC competition is a model of how to develop secure and reliable cryptography in a transparent and collaborative manner. By embracing these principles, we can ensure that our digital world remains secure in the quantum age.

Part II: Diving Deep into Post-Quantum Algorithms

Chapter 4: "Lattice-Based Cryptography: The Frontrunner in Quantum Resistance.

We're zooming in on what many consider the most promising family of PQC algorithms, those based on the fascinating world of mathematical lattices.

Think of lattice-based cryptography as building security around problems in high-dimensional geometry. Instead of relying on factoring large numbers (like RSA) or discrete logarithms (like ECC), we're leveraging the inherent difficulty of finding the "shortest" or "closest" vector in a complex, multi-dimensional grid. It's like trying to find a specific grain of sand on a beach, but the beach is infinitely large and has many dimensions!

(4.1: Fundamentals of Lattice Theory and the Learning With Errors (LWE) Problem):

Instead of focusing on abstract mathematical definitions, we'll use visualizations and analogies to build intuition.

First off: What's a lattice anyway?

(Visualizing a Lattice):

Imagine a perfectly ordered orchard. The trees are planted in a regular grid, with equal spacing between them. This is a good starting point for understanding what a lattice is. Now, imagine extending this grid in all directions, infinitely. That's a 2-dimensional lattice.

More formally, a lattice is a regular, repeating arrangement of points in n-dimensional space. It's a set of all integer linear combinations of a set of linearly independent vectors called the basis vectors.

(What does that *mean*?):

Let's break it down:

- **Basis Vectors:** These are the building blocks of the lattice. They are a set of linearly independent vectors that span the entire lattice. In our orchard analogy, the basis vectors would be the vectors that define the spacing between the trees in each direction.
- **Integer Linear Combinations:** This means that you can reach any point in the lattice by adding integer multiples of the basis vectors. For example, if you have two basis vectors, **v1** and **v2**, then any point in the lattice can be written as a**v1** + b**v2**, where a and b are integers.

Personal Perspective: The first time I saw a visual representation of a high-dimensional lattice, it blew my mind. It's hard to wrap your head around so many dimensions, but the underlying concept is surprisingly simple.

(Code Example: Generating and Visualizing a 2D Lattice):

Let's use Python and Matplotlib to generate and visualize a simple 2-dimensional lattice. This will help you get a better sense of what a lattice looks like.

```python
import numpy as np
import matplotlib.pyplot as plt

def generate_lattice(basis_vectors, limits):
    """Generates a set of lattice points based on the given
basis vectors.

    Args:
        basis_vectors: A list of two basis vectors (NumPy
arrays).
        limits: A tuple specifying the range of integer
multiples for the basis vectors.
            (e.g., (-5, 5) means the multiples will
range from -5 to 5).

    Returns:
        A list of lattice points (NumPy arrays).
    """
    lattice_points = []
    lower_limit, upper_limit = limits
    for i in range(lower_limit, upper_limit + 1):
        for j in range(lower_limit, upper_limit + 1):
```

```python
            point = i * basis_vectors[0] + j *
basis_vectors[1]
            lattice_points.append(point)
    return lattice_points

def visualize_lattice(lattice_points, basis_vectors):
    """Visualizes the lattice points and basis vectors
using matplotlib.

    Args:
        lattice_points: A list of lattice points (NumPy
arrays).
        basis_vectors: A list of two basis vectors (NumPy
arrays).
    """
    x = [point[0] for point in lattice_points]
    y = [point[1] for point in lattice_points]

    plt.figure(figsize=(8, 8))  # Adjust figure size for
better visualization
    plt.scatter(x, y, label="Lattice Points")

    # Plot basis vectors
    for i, vector in enumerate(basis_vectors):
        plt.arrow(0, 0, vector[0], vector[1],
head_width=0.2, head_length=0.3,
                  fc='red', ec='red', label=f"Basis Vector
{i+1}")

    plt.xlabel("X")
    plt.ylabel("Y")
    plt.title("Lattice Points and Basis Vectors")
    plt.grid(True)
    plt.legend()  # Show legend for clarity
    plt.axhline(0, color='black', linewidth=0.5)  # Add
horizontal axis
    plt.axvline(0, color='black', linewidth=0.5)  # Add
vertical axis
    plt.show()

# Define two basis vectors
basis_vectors = [np.array([2, 1]), np.array([1, 3])]

# Define the limits for the integer multiples
limits = (-5, 5)

# Generate lattice points
lattice_points = generate_lattice(basis_vectors, limits)

# Visualize the lattice
```

(Explanation of the Code):

1. **generate_lattice(basis_vectors, limits) Function:** This function takes a list of basis vectors and a range of integer multiples as input and generates a set of lattice points.
2. **visualize_lattice(lattice_points, basis_vectors) Function:** This function takes a list of lattice points and basis vectors as input and visualizes them using Matplotlib.
3. **Basis Vector Definition:** We define two basis vectors ([2, 1] and [1, 3]). These determine the shape and orientation of the lattice.
4. **Limits Definition:** These determine how many multiples of the basis vectors we use to create the lattice points
5. **Lattice Generation and Visualization:** The code generates a set of lattice points and visualizes them, along with the basis vectors.

When you run this code, you'll see a plot of a 2-dimensional lattice, with the basis vectors shown as red arrows. This will give you a visual sense of what a lattice looks like.

(The Learning With Errors (LWE) Problem – Explained in Detail):

Now that we have a basic understanding of lattices, let's dive deeper into the Learning With Errors (LWE) problem. This problem is the foundation of many lattice-based cryptographic schemes.

Imagine that you have a secret point **s** somewhere within the lattice. You also have a set of "noisy" equations that relate to this secret point. These equations aren't perfect; they have some added error or noise. The LWE problem is to find the secret point **s** given these noisy equations.

More formally:

- Let **A** be a random matrix of dimensions m x n (where m > n). The elements of **A** are typically chosen from a uniform distribution modulo some prime number q.
- Let **s** be a secret vector of length n. The elements of **s** are also typically chosen from a uniform distribution modulo q.

- Let **e** be an error vector of length m. The elements of **e** are typically chosen from a discrete Gaussian distribution with a small standard deviation. This means that the errors are small and randomly distributed around zero.
- We are given **A** and $\mathbf{b} = \mathbf{A} \cdot \mathbf{s} + \mathbf{e}$ (where "·" denotes matrix multiplication), and our goal is to recover **s**.

The addition of the error vector **e** makes the LWE problem exponentially harder. Without the error, it would be a simple linear algebra problem. But with the error, it becomes a computationally intractable problem, even for quantum computers.

(Why is LWE hard?):

The hardness of LWE is related to the difficulty of finding the "closest vector" in a lattice. Given a point outside the lattice, finding the closest point in the lattice is a known hard problem. The LWE problem is essentially a disguised version of this closest vector problem.

Personal Perspective: The LWE problem is like trying to find a hidden treasure on a map, but the map is distorted and has lots of misleading information. You have to use all your skills and intuition to filter out the noise and find the true location of the treasure.

We've explored the basic concepts of lattice theory and the Learning With Errors (LWE) problem. In the next sections, we'll build on this foundation to explore specific lattice-based cryptographic schemes, such as CRYSTALS-Kyber and CRYSTALS-Dilithium. You will have a good grasp of how the LWE problem is used to design secure and efficient cryptographic systems.

(Code Illustration: Generating A Matrix and A Vector With Errors):
We can generate the matrix, vector, and error with python as follows,

```python
import numpy as np

def generate_lwe_instance(n, m, q, sigma):
    """Generates a random instance of the Learning With
Errors (LWE) problem.

    Args:
        n: The dimension of the secret vector.
        m: The number of samples (rows in the matrix).
```

```
        q: The modulus.
        sigma: The standard deviation of the discrete
Gaussian distribution for the errors.

    Returns:
        A tuple containing the matrix A, the secret vector
s, the error vector e, and the vector b.
    """
    # Generate the random matrix A
    A = np.random.randint(0, q, size=(m, n))

    # Generate the secret vector s
    s = np.random.randint(0, q, size=n)

    # Generate the error vector e from a discrete Gaussian
distribution
    e = np.round(np.random.normal(0, sigma,
size=m)).astype(int)

    # Calculate b = A @ s + e (mod q)
    b = (A @ s + e) % q

    return A, s, e, b

# Set the parameters
n = 64  # Dimension of the secret vector
m = 128 # Number of samples
q = 1024 # Modulus
sigma = 8 # Standard deviation of the error distribution

# Generate the LWE instance
A, s, e, b = generate_lwe_instance(n, m, q, sigma)

print("Matrix A:\n", A)
print("Secret vector s:\n", s)
print("Error vector e:\n", e)
print("Vector b:\n", b)
```

The point of showing this python code is to display how a matrix and a vector can be formed, but this doesn't provide any real world use without quantum resistant cryptography.

In summary, in understanding fundamentals of cryptography and LWE, we can understand why the matrix A, and vector S can be used to create encryption keys and digital signatures.

(4.2: CRYSTALS-Kyber: A Secure and Efficient Key Encapsulation Mechanism (KEM)):

Think of CRYSTALS-Kyber as a secure "digital envelope" for exchanging secret keys. It's a Key Encapsulation Mechanism (KEM), meaning it's designed to establish a shared secret key between two parties, Alice and Bob, even if an eavesdropper (Eve) is listening. This shared secret can then be used to encrypt further communication using a symmetric-key algorithm like AES.

Kyber stands out due to its balance of strong security, relatively small key sizes, and efficient performance, which led to its selection by NIST for standardization.

(Kyber: Based on Module Learning With Errors (MLWE)):

Kyber builds upon the Module Learning With Errors (MLWE) problem, a variant of the LWE problem we discussed in the previous section. MLWE allows for more efficient implementations and smaller key sizes compared to standard LWE.

(What's "Module" About It?):

In MLWE, instead of working with individual elements (like integers) within the matrix and vectors, we work with *modules*, which are essentially vectors of polynomials. This allows us to pack more information into each element, reducing the overall size of the keys and matrices.

Let's illustrate the high level steps with a simple explanation,

1. Bob samples from the distributions to obtain public key.
2. Alice takes Bob's public key to create secret key.
3. Then, Bob uses the secret key for communication.

(The Key Steps in Kyber:

Let's walk through the key steps in Kyber, focusing on the conceptual flow:

1. **Key Generation (Bob's Side):**
   - Bob generates a secret key **sk** and a public key **pk**. The public key is derived from the secret key using the MLWE problem. This involves generating a random matrix **A** and a noisy vector **b**, such that $b = A * sk + e$, where **e** is a small error vector. The public key **pk** consists of the matrix **A** and the vector **b**. The secret key **sk** is kept private.

2. **Encapsulation (Alice's Side):**
   - Alice wants to send a secret key to Bob. She obtains Bob's public key **pk**.
   - Alice generates a random message **m** (the shared secret key to be established).
   - Alice encrypts the message **m** using Bob's public key **pk**. This involves generating another random matrix **A'** and a noisy vector **e'**, and computing the ciphertext **c** as a function of **A'**, **pk**, **m**, and **e'**. The ciphertext **c** consists of two parts: a vector **u** and a value **v**.

3. **Decapsulation (Bob's Side):**
   - Bob receives the ciphertext **c** from Alice.
   - Bob uses his secret key **sk** to decrypt the ciphertext **c** and recover the message **m** (the shared secret key). This involves computing a value **m'** as a function of **sk** and **c**, and comparing **m'** to **m**. If they are equal, then the decryption is successful.

(Security Properties of Kyber):

Kyber is designed to be resistant to both classical and quantum attacks. Its security is based on the hardness of the MLWE problem, which is believed to be a very difficult problem, even for quantum computers. The key is to build parameters large enough to secure it.

Personal Perspective: What I find particularly appealing about Kyber is its clean and elegant design. It's a relatively simple algorithm that provides strong security and good performance.

(Code Example: High-Level Demonstration (Conceptual) of Kyber Key Generation, Encryption, Decryption):
Since we can not directly implement Kyber (no readily available code), we will illustrate this with a hypothetical example.

```python
        # This is a HIGHLY SIMPLIFIED and INSECURE conceptual
example!
# DO NOT use this in any real-world cryptographic
application.
# It's meant to illustrate the *steps*, not the actual
Kyber implementation.

def generate_keypair():
    """Generates a public key and secret key (insecure
placeholder)."""
    #In reality, this would involve complex lattice-based
math
    secret_key = "This is a fake secret key"  #Placeholder
    public_key = "This is a fake public key" #Placeholder
    return public_key, secret_key

def encrypt(public_key, message):
    """Encrypts a message using the public key (insecure
placeholder)."""
    # In reality, this would involve MLWE operations
    ciphertext = f"Encrypted: {message} with {public_key}"
#Placeholder
    return ciphertext

def decrypt(ciphertext, secret_key):
    """Decrypts the ciphertext using the secret key
(insecure placeholder)."""
    #In reality, this would involve MLWE and error
correction
    if secret_key in ciphertext:
        message = ciphertext.replace("Encrypted: ",
"").replace(f" with {public_key}","") #bad code.

    else:
      message = "Decryption Failure"

    return message

# Example Usage
public_key, secret_key = generate_keypair()

message = "My secret message"
ciphertext = encrypt(public_key, message)
print (f"Ciphertext: {ciphertext}")

decrypted_message = decrypt (ciphertext, secret_key)

print (f"Decrypted Message: {message}")
```

(Important Disclaimers):

- **This code is purely for illustration.** It does *not* implement the actual CRYSTALS-Kyber algorithm.
- **It is HIGHLY INSECURE.** It's designed to show the steps of key exchange, not to provide any real security.
- **Do not use this code for any cryptographic purposes.**

Real-world implementation would involve a much complex code base.

(Areas for Future Discussion):

- **Polynomial Arithmetic:** Kyber relies on polynomial arithmetic in finite fields. This allows for efficient implementation of the MLWE operations.
- **Number Theoretic Transform (NTT):** The NTT is a fast algorithm for performing polynomial multiplication. Kyber uses the NTT to speed up the MLWE operations.

(Conclusion):

CRYSTALS-Kyber is a promising lattice-based Key Encapsulation Mechanism (KEM) that has been selected by NIST for standardization. Its strong security, good performance, and relatively small key sizes make it a good choice for securing communications in the quantum age. While implementing the algorithm from scratch is a complex task, understanding its core principles is essential for cybersecurity professionals who want to protect their systems and data from quantum attacks.

(4.3: CRYSTALS-Dilithium: A Practical Digital Signature Scheme):

Think of CRYSTALS-Dilithium as a secure "digital seal" for your data. It's a digital signature scheme, meaning it allows you to prove that a message is authentic and hasn't been tampered with, even if it's transmitted over an insecure channel. The key here is the ability to prove the message came from a verified source.

Like Kyber, Dilithium was selected by NIST for standardization, highlighting its strong security and practical performance. Its name is cool too.

(Dilithium: Based on Module Short Integer Solution (MSIS)):

Dilithium builds upon a variant of the MLWE problem called the Module Short Integer Solution (MSIS) problem. MSIS is closely related to MLWE, but it's tailored specifically for building signature schemes.

(The Goal of a Digital Signature Scheme):

Before we dive into the details of Dilithium, let's recap the core goals of a digital signature scheme:

- **Authentication:** To prove that a message was indeed signed by the claimed signer.
- **Integrity:** To ensure that the message has not been altered or tampered with since it was signed.
- **Non-Repudiation:** To prevent the signer from denying that they signed the message.

(The Key Steps in Dilithium):

Let's walk through the key steps in Dilithium, again focusing on the conceptual flow:

1. **Key Generation (Signer's Side):**
   - The signer generates a secret key **sk** and a public key **pk**. The public key is derived from the secret key using the MSIS problem.
2. **Signature Generation (Signer's Side):**
   - To sign a message **m**, the signer uses their secret key **sk** to generate a signature **sig**. This involves a complex process that relies on the MSIS problem. The signature depends on both the message and the secret key. It also involves the rejection sampling, meaning that many signatures might need to be generated before an acceptable signature is found.
3. **Signature Verification (Verifier's Side):**

o Anyone with the signer's public key **pk** can verify the signature **sig**. The verification process checks whether the signature is valid for the message **m** and the public key **pk**. If the verification succeeds, then the message is considered authentic and has not been tampered with.

(Rejection Sampling is a Core Part of Dilithium):

A key aspect of Dilithium's design is *rejection sampling*. The signature generation process involves repeatedly sampling random values until a signature is found that meets certain criteria. This is done to prevent information about the secret key from leaking through the signature.

This introduces a bit of variability in the signature generation time. Sometimes it will be fast, and sometimes it will take longer, depending on how many samples are rejected.

Personal Perspective: The concept of rejection sampling was initially confusing to me. It seemed inefficient to throw away so many samples. But then I realized that it's a crucial security mechanism that prevents subtle attacks.

(Code Example: High-Level Demonstration (Conceptual) of Digital Signatures):
Since we can not directly implement Dilithium (no readily available code), we will illustrate this with a hypothetical example.

```
    # This is a HIGHLY SIMPLIFIED and INSECURE conceptual
example!
# DO NOT use this in any real-world cryptographic
application.
# It's meant to illustrate the *steps*, not the actual
Dilithium implementation.

def generate_keypair():
    """Generates a public key and secret key (insecure
placeholder)."""
    secret_key = "Fake Secret Key" #Placeholder
    public_key = "Fake Public Key" #Placeholder
    return public_key, secret_key

def sign_message(message, secret_key):
    """Signs a message using the secret key (insecure
placeholder)."""
```

```
    signature = f"Signed: {message} with
{secret_key}"#Placeholder
    return signature

def verify_signature(message, signature, public_key):
    """Verifies the signature using the public key
(insecure placeholder)."""
    if public_key in signature and message in signature:
        return True
    else:
        return False

# Example Usage
public_key, secret_key = generate_keypair()

message = "This is the message to sign"
signature = sign_message(message, secret_key)

print(f"Message: {message}")
print(f"Signature: {signature}")

is_valid = verify_signature(message, signature, public_key)

if is_valid:
    print("Signature is valid")
else:
    print("Signature is invalid")
```

(Important Disclaimers):

- **This code is purely for illustration.** It does *not* implement the actual CRYSTALS-Dilithium algorithm.
- **It is HIGHLY INSECURE.** It's designed to show the steps of digital signatures, not to provide any real security.
- **Do not use this code for any cryptographic purposes.**

(Security Properties of Dilithium):

Dilithium is designed to be resistant to both classical and quantum attacks. Its security is based on the hardness of the MSIS problem, which is believed to be a very difficult problem, even for quantum computers. Dilithium offers strong security in the face of such threats.

(Key Advantages of Dilithium):

- **Strong Security:** Based on the well-studied MSIS problem.
- **Relatively Small Signatures:** Compared to some other PQC signature schemes.
- **Good Performance:** Offers efficient signature generation and verification.

(Areas for Future Discussion):

- **Fiat-Shamir Transform:** Dilithium uses the Fiat-Shamir transform to convert an identification scheme into a digital signature scheme.
- **Rejection Sampling Details:** A deeper dive into the mathematical details of the rejection sampling process.

(Code Illustration with Elliptic Curve Digital Signature Algorithm (ECDSA) for comparison):

We can present a python code on how to digitally sign a message with ECDSA and compare it to the quantum-resistant methods.

```python
from cryptography.hazmat.primitives import hashes
from cryptography.hazmat.primitives.asymmetric import ec
from cryptography.hazmat.primitives import serialization
from cryptography.hazmat.primitives.asymmetric import utils
from cryptography.hazmat.backends import default_backend
import os

# Generate a private key
private_key = ec.generate_private_key(ec.SECP256R1(),
default_backend())

# Public key serialization (for sharing)
public_key = private_key.public_key()
public_key_bytes = public_key.public_bytes(
    encoding=serialization.Encoding.PEM,
    format=serialization.PublicFormat.SubjectPublicKeyInfo
)

# Message to sign
message = b"This is a test message"

# Signing
hasher = hashes.Hash(hashes.SHA256(), default_backend())
hasher.update(message)
digest = hasher.finalize()

signature = private_key.sign(
```

```
    digest,
    ec.ECDSA(utils.Prehashed(hashes.SHA256()))
)

# Verification
try:
    public_key.verify(
        signature,
        digest,
        ec.ECDSA(utils.Prehashed(hashes.SHA256()))
    )
    print("Signature verification successful!")
except Exception as e:
    print(f"Signature verification failed: {e}")
```

The code above is not quantum-resistant.

(Conclusion):

CRYSTALS-Dilithium is a practical and promising lattice-based digital signature scheme that has been selected by NIST for standardization. Its strong security, relatively small signatures, and good performance make it a strong choice for authenticating data in the quantum age. Understanding Dilithium's core principles is essential for cybersecurity professionals who want to secure their systems and data from quantum attacks.

(4.4: Security Analysis, Performance Benchmarks, and Use Cases):

We've explored the theoretical foundations and conceptual operation of Kyber and Dilithium. Now, we need to critically examine them as tools for securing data in the quantum era.

(Security Analysis: Withstanding the Test of Time (and Attacks)):

Security analysis is the cornerstone of any cryptographic algorithm. It involves subjecting the algorithm to intense scrutiny by experts from around the world to identify any potential weaknesses or vulnerabilities.

(Key Aspects of Security Analysis):

- **Mathematical Analysis:** This involves analyzing the underlying mathematical problems on which the algorithm is based to determine their hardness and resistance to known attacks. This is especially critical for lattice based systems.
- **Cryptanalysis:** This involves attempting to break the algorithm using various attack techniques. This includes both classical and quantum attacks. Cryptanalysis drives security.
- **Formal Verification:** This involves using formal methods to prove that the algorithm meets certain security properties.

(The Security of Kyber and Dilithium):

CRYSTALS-Kyber and CRYSTALS-Dilithium have been subjected to extensive security analysis, and are believed to be resistant to all known attacks, both classical and quantum. Their security is based on the hardness of the MLWE and MSIS problems, which are considered to be among the most promising candidates for post-quantum security. However, no cryptographic algorithm can be proven to be absolutely secure, and it's always possible that new attacks will be discovered in the future. Security must always be assessed.

(Important Caveats):

- **Parameter Selection:** The security of Kyber and Dilithium depends on the careful selection of parameters, such as the size of the matrices and vectors, the modulus, and the standard deviation of the error distribution. Choosing weak parameters can make the algorithms vulnerable to attack.
- **Implementation Security:** Even if the algorithm itself is secure, a poor implementation can introduce vulnerabilities. It's essential to implement Kyber and Dilithium carefully and to follow best practices for secure coding.

(Performance Benchmarks: Speed and Efficiency in the Real World):

Security is important, but it's not the only consideration. Cryptographic algorithms also need to be efficient enough to be used in real-world applications. Performance benchmarks measure the speed and efficiency of the algorithms in terms of key generation, encryption, decryption, signature generation, and signature verification.

(Performance Metrics):

- **Key Generation Time:** The time it takes to generate a public key and secret key.
- **Encryption/Decapsulation Time (Kyber):** The time it takes to encrypt a message (encapsulation) and decrypt a ciphertext (decapsulation).
- **Signature Generation Time (Dilithium):** The time it takes to generate a digital signature.
- **Signature Verification Time (Dilithium):** The time it takes to verify a digital signature.
- **Key Size:** The size of the public key and secret key.
- **Ciphertext Size (Kyber):** The size of the ciphertext.
- **Signature Size (Dilithium):** The size of the digital signature.

(Performance of Kyber and Dilithium):

CRYSTALS-Kyber and CRYSTALS-Dilithium offer good performance, making them suitable for a wide range of applications. They are generally faster than other PQC algorithms, and their key and ciphertext/signature sizes are relatively small. The actual performance depends on the specific implementation and the hardware platform, but they are generally considered to be practical and efficient.

(Use Cases: Securing the Digital World with Kyber and Dilithium):

Finally, let's consider some of the specific use cases where CRYSTALS-Kyber and CRYSTALS-Dilithium can be used to secure the digital world:

- **Secure Communication:**
  - Securing email communication with PQC-enabled email clients.
  - Securing messaging apps with PQC-enabled encryption protocols.
  - Securing voice and video calls with PQC-enabled key exchange mechanisms.
- **Digital Signatures:**
  - Authenticating software updates to prevent malware attacks.
  - Signing documents and contracts to ensure their authenticity and integrity.

- o Securing code signing processes to prevent unauthorized modifications.
- **Key Exchange:**
  - o Securing web browsing with PQC-enabled TLS protocols.
  - o Securing VPN connections with PQC-enabled key exchange mechanisms.
  - o Securing IoT devices with PQC-enabled authentication and encryption.
- **Cloud Security:**
  - o Protecting sensitive data stored in the cloud with PQC-enabled encryption.
  - o Securing virtual machines and containers with PQC-enabled authentication.
- **Block Chain:**
  - o Making sure new block chains are PQC secured.

Personal Perspective: The versatility of Kyber and Dilithium is what makes them so exciting. They're not just theoretical algorithms; they're practical tools that can be used to solve real-world security problems.

(Conclusion):

CRYSTALS-Kyber and CRYSTALS-Dilithium represent a significant step forward in securing our digital infrastructure against quantum attacks. Their strong security, good performance, and versatile use cases make them a leading choice for post-quantum cryptography. While there are still challenges to overcome, such as the need for standardization and widespread implementation, these algorithms offer a promising path towards a quantum-resistant future.

Chapter 5: Alternative PQC Approaches: Code-Based and Hash-Based Cryptography

Alternative PQC Approaches: Code-Based and Hash-Based Cryptography." While lattice-based cryptography currently leads the pack, code-based and hash-based schemes offer compelling alternatives with unique strengths and design philosophies. We will examine code-based and hash-based algorithms strengths, weaknesses, and suitability for different applications.

It's like diversifying your investment portfolio. You wouldn't put all your eggs in one basket, right? Similarly, in cryptography, it's prudent to have multiple algorithms based on different mathematical principles, in case one approach is compromised.

(5.1: Classic McEliece: Leveraging Coding Theory for Quantum-Safe Encryption):

Imagine sending a package across the country. You wouldn't just throw the contents into an unpadded box, right? You'd carefully pack it with protective materials to prevent damage during transit. Error-correcting codes do something similar for digital information, adding redundancy that allows us to recover the original message even if some bits are corrupted. Classic McEliece turns this principle into an encryption scheme.

(The Core Idea: Hiding a Goppa Code):

The McEliece cryptosystem is a public-key encryption scheme based on the difficulty of decoding *random* linear codes. However, decoding arbitrary codes is hard. However, McEliece introduces *Goppa codes*.

The secret sauce in McEliece is the use of *Goppa codes*, which are a special class of linear codes that have efficient decoding algorithms. The public key doesn't reveal the original Goppa code directly; instead, it presents a disguised version. This disguised code looks like a random, unstructured code, making it difficult to decode without knowing the secret key.

(What's a Linear Code?):

Before delving into the details, let's clarify what a linear code is. A linear code is a set of codewords (valid messages) that form a linear subspace. This means that if you add two codewords together, the result is also a codeword. Linear codes can be described by a generator matrix **G**, which is a matrix whose rows form a basis for the code. Any codeword can be obtained by multiplying a message vector by the generator matrix.

(How McEliece Works - A Step-by-Step Breakdown):

Let's walk through the key steps of the McEliece cryptosystem:

1. **Key Generation (Bob's Side):**
   o **Choose a Goppa Code (G):** Bob selects a Goppa code **G**, which has efficient decoding algorithm. This code will form the base.
   o **Random Invertible Matrix (S):** Bob picks a random, invertible matrix **S**. This will scramble the rows of the matrix to hide the secret key.
   o **Random Permutation Matrix (P):** Bob also generates a random permutation matrix **P**. This will simply permute the columns.
   o **Public Key (G'):** Bob makes public **G' = SGP** as the public key.
   o **Bob's Secret Key (S, G, P):** Bob will then keep the secret matrix **S**, code **G**, and the permutation matrix **P**.
2. **Encryption (Alice's Side):**
   o **Obtain Public Key:** Alice finds Bob's public key **G'**.
   o **Encode Message:** Alice puts the message as **m**, and encodes it as a code word.
   o **Introduce Error:** To introduce a set of code for the error, Alice adds an error vector to the code word **e**.
   o **Bob's Cipher text:** Alice sends over **c = mG' + e**.
3. **Decryption (Bob's Side):**
   o **Multiply By Permutation Matrix:** Bob receives **c**, then performs **cP^-1**, to undo the public key.

- o **Removing invertible Matrix:** After that, Bob decodes the message using **S^-1**, to reveal the message.

(Why is McEliece Quantum-Resistant?):

The security of McEliece is based on the difficulty of decoding *random* linear codes. While decoding Goppa codes is easy with the secret key, decoding a *random* linear code is believed to be a very difficult problem, even for quantum computers. No efficient quantum algorithm is known for solving this problem.

(Trade-offs of McEliece):

The major drawback is the large key size. This is not ideal for constrained devices. However, McEliece is designed to be resistant to quantum attacks.

Personal Perspective: I admire McEliece's simplicity and elegance. It's a very old algorithm, yet it has withstood the test of time. This proves its excellent design, and security.

(Code Illustration (simplified with explanation):

```python
    import numpy as np

def generate_goppa_code(n, k, t):
    """Generates a random binary Goppa code.
    Note: this part is greatly simplified, a real
implementation uses more complex polynomials.

    Args:
        n: Code length.
        k: Message length.
        t: Error correction capability.

    Returns:
        A generator matrix (numpy array).
    """
    # Simplification: a random matrix acts as the Goppa
code
    G = np.random.randint(0, 2, size=(k, n))
    return G

def create_keypair(n, k, t):
    """Creates a McEliece key pair.
```

```
    Args:
        n: Code length.
        k: Message length.
        t: Error correction capability.

    Returns:
        A tuple containing the public key (G'), and the
private key (S, G, P).
    """

    # 1. Generate the Goppa code G
    G = generate_goppa_code(n, k, t)

    # 2. Generate random invertible matrix S (k x k)
    S = np.random.randint(0, 2, size=(k, k))
    while np.linalg.det(S) == 0:  # Ensure S is invertible
(over binary field)
        S = np.random.randint(0, 2, size=(k, k))

    # 3. Generate random permutation matrix P (n x n)
    P = np.random.permutation(np.eye(n)) #This can be
represented as an array to reduce key size.

    # 4. Calculate the public key G' = S * G * P
    G_prime = S @ G @ P

    #Private code, used to reverse.
    return G_prime, (S, G, P)

def add_error(codeword, t, n):
    """Adds 't' random errors to a codeword."""
    error_indices = np.random.choice(n, size=t,
replace=False) # 't' positions to flip
    error_vector = np.zeros(n)
    error_vector[error_indices] = 1
    noisy_codeword = (codeword + error_vector) % 2  #
Binary field arithmetic
    return noisy_codeword

def encrypt(public_key, message, t, n):
    """Encrypts a message using McEliece.

    Args:
        public_key: The public key (G').
        message: The message to encrypt (as a numpy array,
length k).
        t: The error correction capability
        n: Code length
```

```python
    Returns:
        The ciphertext (numpy array).
    """
    #Need to zero-pad here because encoding a message into
Goppa code with code length must equal length k
    if len(message) < public_key.shape[0]:
        pad_size = public_key.shape[0] - len(message)
        padded_message = np.concatenate([message,
np.zeros(pad_size)])
    else:
        padded_message = message

    codeword = (padded_message @ public_key) % 2 # Linear
code word.

    error_positions = add_error(codeword, t, n)

    return error_positions

def decrypt(ciphertext, private_key):
    """Decrypts the ciphertext using the private key."""
    S, G, P = private_key
    # Undo the permutation
    permuted_ciphertext = ciphertext @ np.linalg.inv(P)

    # The actual decoding (undoing Goppa code) is too
complicated to implement here.
    # Instead, we just zero out the errors since this is a
simplification

    # Undo the scrambling (S matrix) - this requires the
pseudo-inverse
    # Note: this is just for demonstration, decoding
algorithm for Goppa is too complex to show.
    plaintext = permuted_ciphertext @ np.linalg.inv(S)

    #The above is an illustration.
    return plaintext

def generate_binary_message(k):
  """Generates binary messages.

  Args:
    k: The bit length to generate the messages.

  Returns:
      The binary message in form of array.
  """
  message = np.random.randint(0, 2, k)
  return message
```

```
# Parameters
n = 10   # Code length (the block length of the code)
k = 5    # Message length (the dimension of the code)
t = 1    # Error correction capability (number of errors
that can be corrected)

# 1. Key Generation
public_key, private_key = create_keypair(n, k, t)
print ("The public key is:", public_key)
print ("The private key is:", private_key)

# 2. Encryption
message_vector = generate_binary_message(k)   # Example
message (binary numpy array).  Must be length k or smaller
ciphertext = encrypt(public_key, message_vector, t, n)

# 3. Decryption
print("Ciphertext:", ciphertext)

plaintext = decrypt(ciphertext, private_key)
print("Plaintext after decryption:", plaintext)

print("Original Message:", message_vector)
print("Decrypted Message:", plaintext)
```

The code above is an approximation of what happens in practice,

(Code Disclaimers):

- **DO NOT USE THIS FOR REAL ENCRYPTION!**
- This code does not implement actual Goppa code decoding, so it is insecure
- This illustration helps understand the code.

(What We Avoided):

To keep this accessible, we skipped over much of the complexity of real-world McEliece implementations. The core ideas are preserved, and the python code shows how an act of coding, un-coding and adding noise provides the means for encryption.

(In Conclusion):

Classic McEliece offers a compelling path to quantum-safe encryption, leveraging the well-established principles of coding theory. This has been a journey into some very complicated maths, with some help of python code.

(5.2: SPHINCS+: Stateless Hash-Based Signatures for Uncompromising Security):

Imagine needing to sign thousands of documents, but you're working from a device that could be compromised at any time. You wouldn't want to risk your secret key getting stolen, right? SPHINCS+ is designed for scenarios where key security and lack of state are vital.

(The Problem with Stateful Signatures (Revisited):

Traditional digital signature schemes, like RSA or ECDSA, often require the signer to maintain a secret state, such as a counter or a set of pre-generated keys. This state must be carefully protected, because if it's compromised or lost, the security of the entire system is at risk. In real-world implementation, it might be hard to ensure.

This is difficult in the case of securing an airplane through code. So, we need a stateless solution,

(SPHINCS+: Stateless Simplicity):

SPHINCS+ (pronounced "Sphinx Plus") solves this problem by using a stateless design. The signer doesn't need to store any secret state. The signature is generated solely from the message and the signer's secret key. It makes SPHINCS+ robust.

(How SPHINCS+ Achieves Statelessness:

SPHINCS+ achieves statelessness through a clever combination of hash functions and a Merkle tree. It uses the hash functions are used as one way function, with each of the children to create the authentication paths.

(Breaking Down the Key Components):

To understand SPHINCS+, let's break down its key components:

- **Cryptographic Hash Functions:** These are the workhorses of SPHINCS+. A cryptographic hash function takes an input of any size and produces a fixed-size output (the hash value). The hash function should be one-way (difficult to reverse) and collision-resistant (difficult to find two different inputs that produce the same hash value).
- **Merkle Tree:** A Merkle tree is a binary tree where each node contains the hash of its children. The leaves of the tree contain the hashes of the messages that are being signed. Used to generate signatures.
- **One-Time Signature (OTS) Scheme:** SPHINCS+ uses a one-time signature (OTS) scheme to sign each leaf of the Merkle tree. An OTS scheme can only be used to sign a single message securely. For example, it can be WOTS+.
- **Hyper-Tree Structure:** The structure combines many trees, to allow lower signature sizes.

(The Signature Generation Process (Simplified):

Let's outline the signature generation process in SPHINCS+, greatly simplified for clarity:

1. **Generate a Root Hash:** Use a secret key to generate a root hash.
2. **Hash the Message:** Compute the hash of the message you want to sign.
3. **Derive Authentication Path:** Reveal a portion of the Merkle tree to prove you hold a message, and not a fraud
4. **Sign With One Time Signature:** One time signature scheme, to secure the document.

(The Signature Verification Process (Simplified):

1. **Use the Public Key to Get the Root:** Use the root to discover it's been tampered with.
2. **Use the Authentication Path to Get to the Root:** Compare your new root to the original root, and if they are same, the file checks out.

(Why is SPHINCS+ Quantum-Resistant?):

The security of SPHINCS+ relies on the security of the underlying hash function. Cryptographic hash functions are generally believed to be resistant to attacks from quantum computers. There's no known quantum algorithm that can efficiently break the one-way or collision-resistance properties of hash functions. With these quantum properties, the result makes the SPHINCS+ algorithm to be secure.

Personal Perspective: What I appreciate most about SPHINCS+ is its elegant combination of simplicity and security. By relying on well-established hash functions and a clever tree structure, it achieves a high level of security without the need for complex mathematical assumptions. The reliance on SHA also is important.

(Code Example: Hashing and signing of data):

```python
        import hashlib
import os

# Simulate a secret key (in reality, this would be securely
generated and stored)
secret_key = os.urandom(32)   # 256 bits of random data

def hash_message(message):
    """Hashes a message using SHA-256."""
    hasher = hashlib.sha256(message.encode('utf-8'))
    return hasher.digest()

def generate_signature(message, secret_key):
    """Generates a signature (simplified, NOT SPHINCS+)."""
    #  In actual implementation, we generate many one time
signatures, then we secure that,
    # This process, instead, shows simple signing.
    hashed_message = hash_message(message)
    combined = secret_key + hashed_message
    signature = hashlib.sha256(combined).digest()
    return signature

def verify_signature(message, signature, public_key):
    """Verifies a signature (simplified, NOT SPHINCS+)."""

    #The public key is used to retrieve the root.
    #Use the path to see that we have the right root.

    hashed_message = hash_message(message)
    combined = public_key + hashed_message
    expected_signature = hashlib.sha256(combined).digest()
    return signature == expected_signature
```

```
# In actual SPHINCS+, a tree structure and one-time
signatures to achieve statelessness
# In particular, W-OTS.

# Example Usage
message = "This is a message to sign."
#In real systems, this is generated from a tree.
public_key = os.urandom(32)  #In reality, this is generated
from a tree.

signature = generate_signature(message, secret_key)
is_valid = verify_signature(message, signature, public_key)

print(f"Message: {message}")
print(f"Signature: {signature.hex()}") # Convert bytes to a
hex string for readability

if is_valid:
    print("Signature is valid.")
else:
    print("Signature is invalid.")
```

This code shows some signing.

(Tradeoffs with SPHINCS+):

Key tradeoffs are it's very expensive signature size, and the performance is slower than that of ECDSA.

(In Conclusion):

SPHINCS+ provides a compelling approach to quantum-safe digital signatures, trading off signature size and performance for uncompromising security and statelessness. The properties of SPHINCS+ makes the digital algorithm to be secure, and safe from the use of quantum algorithms. The algorithm, combined with the SHA hash, this creates SPHINCS+! We will now look at how SPHINCS+, can be used for different things.

(5.3: Algorithm Strengths, Weaknesses, and Suitability for Different Applications):

Now that we've explored Classic McEliece and SPHINCS+, we need to weigh their pros and cons to determine where each algorithm shines.

It's like evaluating different tools in a workshop. A hammer is great for driving nails, but it's not the right tool for delicate soldering work. Similarly, each PQC algorithm has its own strengths and weaknesses, making it better suited for certain applications than others. There is no one-size-fits-all solution!

Let's start by summarizing the strengths and weaknesses of each algorithm.

(Classic McEliece: Strengths and Weaknesses):

- **Strengths:**
    - **Long Track Record:** The McEliece cryptosystem has been around for over 40 years and has withstood extensive cryptanalysis. This provides a high degree of confidence in its long-term security.
    - **Underlying security not related to number theory:** Almost every other code is derived from number theory, posing a risk.
    - **Resistance to Quantum Attacks:** The security of McEliece is based on the difficulty of decoding random linear codes, a problem believed to be hard even for quantum computers.
- **Weaknesses:**
    - **Large Key Sizes:** McEliece has significantly larger key sizes than other public-key cryptosystems, including lattice-based schemes. This can be a concern for applications with limited storage or bandwidth.
    - **Slower encryption:** the code performs at a slower rate than others.

(SPHINCS+: Strengths and Weaknesses):

- **Strengths:**

- o **Statelessness:** SPHINCS+ doesn't require the signer to maintain any secret state, making it highly robust against key compromise. This is a major advantage in scenarios where key security is paramount.
  - o **Provable Security:** The security of SPHINCS+ can be mathematically proven based on the security of the underlying hash function. This provides a high degree of confidence in its security.
  - o **Relies on Hash Functions:** The relied algorithm has been reviewed for its use in quantum properties.
- **Weaknesses:**
  - o **Large Signatures:** SPHINCS+ has relatively large signatures compared to other signature schemes. This can be a concern for applications with limited bandwidth.
  - o **Performance:** the system performs slower than some cryptographic methods.

(The Suitability Matrix: Matching Algorithms to Applications):

So, which algorithm should you choose for your specific application? Here's a guide:

- **Classic McEliece:**
  - o **Best Suited For:**
    - ▪ Archival Encryption: Storing data that needs to remain confidential for decades, even if quantum computers become a reality. The large key sizes are less of a concern for archival storage.
    - ▪ Scenarios Where Key Security is Critical: Where resistance to key compromise is a high priority.
- **SPHINCS+:**
  - o **Best Suited For:**
    - ▪ Stateless Devices: Devices that cannot reliably store state, such as some types of IoT devices.
    - ▪ Code Signing: Where key compromise is a major concern. The statelessness of SPHINCS+ makes it difficult for attackers to forge signatures, even if they gain access to the signing key.
    - ▪ Blockchains and Cryptocurrencies: The algorithm is safe from the loss of code, so, it is more secure for securing block chains.

Personal Perspective: In the end, the choice of which PQC algorithm to use depends on a careful analysis of the specific requirements of your application. There is no one-size-fits-all solution. You need to weigh the trade-offs between security, performance, and key/signature size to make the best choice. This analysis is key!

(Code Example: Hashing with SHA-256 and HMAC):

While we can't directly compare the performance of McEliece and SPHINCS+ because we can't implement the code, we can illustrate the concept of using hash functions in a more secure way by showing how to use HMAC (Hash-based Message Authentication Code) with SHA-256. HMAC provides message authentication by combining a secret key with the hash of the message.

```python
import hashlib
import hmac
import os

def generate_secure_key(length=32):
    """Generates a cryptographically secure random key."""
    return os.urandom(length)

def calculate_hmac(key, message):
    """Calculates the HMAC-SHA256 of a message using a
secret key."""
    hmac_obj = hmac.new(key, message.encode('utf-8'),
hashlib.sha256)
    return hmac_obj.digest()

def verify_hmac(key, message, hmac_value):
    """Verifies the HMAC-SHA256 of a message against a
given HMAC value."""
    expected_hmac = calculate_hmac(key, message)
    return hmac.compare_digest(hmac_value, expected_hmac)
# Secure comparison

# Example Usage
#In reality, you would store the key, with access only to
authorized users.
secret_key = generate_secure_key()
message = "This is a secret message."

hmac_value = calculate_hmac(secret_key, message)
is_authentic = verify_hmac(secret_key, message, hmac_value)

print(f"Message: {message}")
```

```
print(f"HMAC Value: {hmac_value.hex()}") #Convert bytes to
hex

if is_authentic:
    print("Message is authentic.")
else:
    print("Message is not authentic!")
```

This code doesn't illustrate key strengths and weakness, but instead, shows use of security with HMAC.

(Conclusion):

Classic McEliece and SPHINCS+ offer valuable alternative approaches to quantum-safe cryptography. Code-based offers a time tested code based encryption scheme, and SPHINCS+ a stateless protocol to prevent key compromise. Make sure to research what is best suited to your needs!

Chapter 6: (Optional) Lessons Learned: The Case of Isogeny-Based Cryptography and SIKE

Think of SIKE as a promising new architectural design for a skyscraper. It looked elegant and efficient on paper, but when subjected to real-world stresses, it crumbled. While disappointing, the failure of SIKE provides valuable insights into the challenges of building quantum-resistant cryptography.

(6.1: A discussion of SIKE and the reasons why it was broken):

Think of SIKE as a beautiful, modern bridge that tragically collapsed shortly after opening. Understanding why it failed is crucial for designing stronger, more resilient bridges in the future. We need to look at SIKE and the lessons it can teach us.

(What is Isogeny-Based Cryptography (Explained Again):

First, let's revisit the concept of isogeny-based cryptography. It's a branch of PQC that relies on the difficulty of finding *isogenies* between elliptic curves. To better understand, we will dive into it.

1. **What are elliptic curves?** The elliptic curves rely on complex equation for the curve.
2. **What is Isogeny?:** Map between the curves.

The goal of the attacker, is to reveal the key with such finite properties.

(SIKE: A Promising Candidate):

Supersingular Isogeny Key Encapsulation (SIKE) was a prominent candidate in the NIST PQC standardization process. It had some appealing features:

- **Small Key Sizes:** Compared to other PQC algorithms, SIKE offered relatively small key sizes. This made it attractive for resource-constrained devices and applications where bandwidth is limited.
- **Relatively new, and promising security strength:** The code has been around for sometime, with no known exploits, increasing its security.

Personal Perspective: The small key sizes of SIKE were particularly attractive. In a world of ever-increasing data volumes, minimizing key sizes is a major advantage. The small size made it easier to transmit.

(The Attack(s) on SIKE (Simplified):

In July 2022, the cryptographic community was rocked by the news that SIKE had been broken. Multiple attacks were published that could break SIKE in practice, rendering it insecure. The most devastating attack was developed by Christophe Petit, Barbara Schwermer, and Wessel van Woerden.

(The High-Level Explanation of the Attack):

The Petit et al. attack exploited a weakness in the *action of torsion points* on the isogeny graph. To simplify:

1. **Torsion points with small parameters:** The exploit related to points in the curve, that did not have enough complexity, leaving points of weakness to derive the code.

These are the following results:

- Small Key: Small key sizes were broken.
- Small code: Similar results were achieved.
- Easy to work on: A code that has been broken more than the rest.

(A More Technical Overview):

For those with a stronger mathematical background, here's a slightly more technical overview of the attack:

- The attack uses a technique called *meet-in-the-middle* to efficiently search for the secret key.
- The attack exploits the *smoothness* of the endomorphism ring of the elliptic curve.
- The attack reduces the search space for the secret key by exploiting the structure of the isogeny graph and its torsion points.

Personal Perspective: The attack on SIKE was a masterclass in cryptanalysis. It demonstrated the importance of understanding the subtle mathematical properties of cryptographic algorithms and how they can be exploited to break the system.

(The Lessons Learned (and Re-Learned):

The breaking of SIKE provides several valuable lessons for cybersecurity professionals and cryptographers:

1. *No Algorithm is Ever Truly "Proven" Secure:* The security of any cryptographic algorithm is based on the assumption that no one knows how to break it *yet*. There's always a possibility that a new attack will be discovered, even after years of scrutiny.
2. *Small Parameters Don't Always Mean Greater Efficiency:* SIKE's small key sizes was one of its attractions. However, it also contributed to its downfall. Because code can be more simply broken with smaller parts.
3. *Defense in Depth is Key:* Never rely on a single cryptographic algorithm to protect your systems and data. Use a variety of algorithms to provide defense in depth. So, if one algorithm falls the rest will fall too.

(Code Example: Illustrating "Meet in the Middle Attack":

```
        import hashlib
import itertools
import time

def hash_function(data):
    """A simple hashing function (e.g., SHA256)."""
    return hashlib.sha256(data.encode('utf-8')).hexdigest()

def simplified_meet_in_the_middle(target_hash,
known_prefix_length=1, search_space_size=1000):
```

```python
    """Illustrates Meet-in-the-Middle concept (HIGHLY
SIMPLIFIED!).

    Args:
        target_hash: The hash we are trying to find a
collision for.
        known_prefix_length: Length of known initial part
of the potential secret.
        search_space_size: Number of pre-computed hashes to
store.

    Returns:
        A tuple: (potential secret, attack time) or (None,
None) if not found.
    """
    start_time = time.time()
    # Phase 1: Pre-compute hashes of known prefixes + short
random strings
    prefix = "known"[:known_prefix_length] # Use some
prefix
    hash_table = {}
    for i in range(search_space_size):
        candidate = prefix + str(i)
        hashed_candidate = hash_function(candidate)
        hash_table[hashed_candidate] = candidate

    # Phase 2: Search for a match by working from the other
end
    # Imagine a simplified scenario where we can slightly
modify the TARGET
    # The goal is to meet in the middle: find some x and y
where H(x) = modify(target_hash, y)

    for j in range(search_space_size): # Limited size of
the "suffix" to check
        possible_secret = str(j)
        # Create a function that "modifies" the target, in
reality this is finding a collision
        modified_hash = hash_function(possible_secret)

        if modified_hash in hash_table:
            full_candidate = hash_table[modified_hash] + "
+ " + possible_secret
            attack_time = time.time() - start_time
            return full_candidate, attack_time # Found a
match

    return None, None

# Try to find a collision for this example
```

```
target_value = "SecretValue"
example_hash = hash_function(target_value)

collision, attack_duration =
simplified_meet_in_the_middle(example_hash,
known_prefix_length=1)

if collision:
    print(f"Meet-in-the-Middle collision found: {collision}
in {attack_duration:.4f} seconds")
else:
    print("No collision found within the limited search
space.")
```

Important Disclaimer: This is an abstracted sample; isogenies are much more complex.

(A Summary):

By better understanding SIKE, we can build a secure code, and understand code properties for years to come. Now we can analyze and understand PQC, and new cryptographic methods as well.

(6.2: Why the broken algorithm helps):

Imagine a structural engineer studying a collapsed bridge. The collapse itself is tragic, but the analysis of *why* it collapsed can lead to better designs, stronger materials, and safer bridges in the future. Similarly, the breaking of SIKE provides critical insights that can improve the design and analysis of PQC algorithms.

(The Unexpected Benefits of Failure):

The breaking of SIKE, while disappointing, has several positive consequences:

1. ***It Validates the Importance of Open Cryptography:** The open and transparent nature of the NIST PQC process allowed the cryptographic community to quickly analyze SIKE, identify its weaknesses, and develop effective attacks. This demonstrates the value of open cryptography, where algorithms are publicly

available for scrutiny. Imagine if SIKE was proprietary and no-one could verify the algorithms.

2. *It Drives Innovation in Cryptanalysis:* The attacks on SIKE introduced new techniques for analyzing isogeny-based cryptosystems. These techniques can be used to evaluate the security of other isogeny-based algorithms and potentially identify new vulnerabilities. It helps people build more secure codes.

3. *It Forces Us to Re-Evaluate Our Assumptions:* The breaking of SIKE challenged some of the assumptions that were being made about the security of isogeny-based cryptography. It forced researchers to re-evaluate their models and look for new ways to strengthen the algorithms. By reviewing our past work, we can understand how to move forward.

(Specific Lessons Learned from SIKE):

Let's dive into the specific lessons that we can learn from the SIKE experience:

1. ***Torsion Point Exploitation:** The attack on SIKE highlighted the importance of carefully analyzing the action of torsion points on the isogeny graph. Future isogeny-based cryptosystems need to be designed to prevent this type of attack. A vulnerability will be taken advantage of, if there are weak points in the code.

2. ***The Dangers of Overconfidence:** The SIKE team was very confident in the security of their algorithm, and they may have been less open to criticism than they should have been. The breaking of SIKE serves as a reminder that no cryptographic algorithm is ever truly "proven" secure, and it's important to be humble and open to feedback. All codes can be broken, and people need to account for that.

3. ***The Need for Diverse Approaches:** The reliance on a single family of elliptic curves had a very strong implication for what had happened.

Personal Perspective: It's a good reminder that in cryptography, you can't just rely on theoretical proofs. You also need to subject your algorithms to practical cryptanalysis. What you need to consider is how the code does something!

(How the SIKE Failure Benefits Cybersecurity Professionals):

While the breaking of SIKE was a setback for isogeny-based cryptography, it ultimately benefits cybersecurity professionals by:

- **Raising Awareness:** The SIKE incident has raised awareness of the importance of PQC and the need to prepare for the quantum threat. It reminds people why its important.
- **Improving Algorithm Selection:** The lessons learned from SIKE can help cybersecurity professionals make better decisions about which PQC algorithms to use to protect their systems and data. By selecting diversified code and multiple code streams, the risk is lower that code will be broken.
- **Promoting Better Implementation Practices:** We need to implement, audit and test our cryptography.

(Code Example: Simulating Cryptographic Hash (Collision Vulnerability)):

While we cannot illustrate isogeny, we can see the problems of using the algorithm by reverse engineering the process:

```python
import hashlib
import random

def generate_short_strings(length, num_strings):
  """Generates number of different strings.

  Args:
      length: The length of each string.
      num_strings: The number of strings to generate.

  Returns:
      A list of randomly generated strings.
  """
  strings = []
  for _ in range(num_strings):
    characters = 'abcdef0123456789'
    string = ''.join(random.choice(characters) for _ in
range(length))
    strings.append(string)
  return strings

def find_hash_collision(num_attempts=10000):
    """Attempts to find a collision in SHA-256 (simplified
illustration).
```

```
    Demonstrates Birthday Paradox-like vulnerabilities (NOT
a practical attack).

    Args:
        num_attempts: The number of strings to generate for
testing.

    Returns:
        A tuple: (string1, string2) if collision is found,
(None, None) otherwise.
    """
    generated_hashes = {}  # Store hashes to check for
collision
    strings = generate_short_strings(5, num_attempts)
#Trying codes for 5 permutations, making easy to compute.

    for string in strings:
        hash_value = hashlib.sha256(string.encode('utf-
8')).hexdigest()
        if hash_value in generated_hashes:
            return generated_hashes[hash_value], string  #
Collision found!
        else:
            generated_hashes[hash_value] = string

    return None, None # No collision found

# Try to find a collision
string1, string2 = find_hash_collision()

if string1:
    print(f"Collision found! String 1: {string1}, String 2:
{string2}")
    hash1 = hashlib.sha256(string1.encode('utf-
8')).hexdigest()
    hash2 = hashlib.sha256(string2.encode('utf-
8')).hexdigest()
    print(f"Hash Value: {hash1}")
    print(f"Hash Value: {hash2}")
else:
    print("No collision found after the given attempts.")
```

The code has the power to verify if a message is not secured properly.

(Why This Code Matters):

The more diverse code, the better! Diversification has more protection. Security is paramount!

(In Conclusion):

The failure of SIKE is a valuable learning opportunity for the cybersecurity community. By understanding why SIKE was broken, we can improve the design and analysis of PQC algorithms and build a more secure future. While no one sets out to see their hard work fail, there's tremendous benefit in understanding cryptographic failures to design more robust systems.

(6.3: What we need to know about this):

Imagine receiving a safety bulletin after a major accident. It wouldn't just describe what happened; it would tell you *what you need to do differently* to prevent similar accidents in the future. This section is our cybersecurity safety bulletin, based on the SIKE experience.

(Putting SIKE into Context):

Let's revisit that SIKE is not just a single incident, but a part of code in the ever evolving field of cybersecurity. If anything, what has happened should be seen as an alert on what future problems could be. In summary, the core principles will always remain key.

(Key Takeaways for Actionable Defenses:

To secure that we can protect our defenses from future algorithm exploits, here are key takeaways,

1. *Stay Informed About PQC:* In order to stay ahead of PQC, one must continuously be in the look out for new updates and information to secure themselves. The best way to do this is through a subscription to code.
2. *Utilize Code Diversification:* Always secure yourself with multiple codes.
3. *Key Security:* In real code, you will need a well defined public and private key code. This creates key authentication, for an improved code.
4. *Follow Code Procedure:* You always want a code that has been tested and known to work well.

(Code Review for PQC Systems):

- **Well documented:*** Always look for code that is easy to understand and read, and has proper information on its build. If code is hard to read, it might be hard to know if that system is really secure.
- **Open Source:*** In many of the real world examples that we covered, we wanted the data for the code to be open. Having more people working and reviewing the code will greatly improve it's ability to be successful.

(Summary of What is Important From Chapter 6).

The point of this chapter is not to get down on anyone, or to discredit new forms of cryptography and systems. However, for code to be strong, it must be reliable in different forms.
These points were proven with the breaking of SIKE.

(What to Consider):

1. A review on code.
2. Implementation and data must be available
3. Code must be flexible.
4. Open-source
5. Longstanding

(Real Time Python: Key Handling):
Even with an advanced code, keys will always need to be a point of focus. The python code illustrates that we must, protect the key, or else, the system will not work.

```python
    import os
from cryptography.fernet import Fernet

def generate_key():
    """Generates a Fernet key (symmetric encryption)."""
    key = Fernet.generate_key()
    return key

def save_key(key, filename="secret.key"):
    """Saves the key to a file."""
    with open(filename, "wb") as key_file:
        key_file.write(key)
    print(f"Key saved to {filename}")

def load_key(filename="secret.key"):
```

```python
    """Loads the key from a file."""
    try:
        with open(filename, "rb") as key_file:
            key = key_file.read()
        return key
    except FileNotFoundError:
        print(f"Error: Key file {filename} not found.")
        return None

# --- Example Usage ---
# 1. Generate Key (Only do this ONCE)
new_key = generate_key()
save_key(new_key)

# 2. Load Key (For encryption/decryption)
loaded_key = load_key()

if loaded_key:
    print("Key loaded successfully.")
else:
    print("Key loading failed.")
```

(Important security note: for safety, this should be for demonstration purposes only)

(Important Reminders):

- Keys need to be rotated as often as possible
- Keys are not to be shared

With this high security code, it's much harder for things to be hacked.

(In Conclusion:)

The SIKE incident is not a reason to give up on PQC. Instead, it's a valuable lesson in what NOT to do, it highlights the importance of open standards and public scrutiny, and it reinforces the need for defense in depth. By learning from the mistakes of the past, we can build a more secure future for our code, with all the tools from code, to safety regulations.

Part III: Implementing and Deploying Post-Quantum Solutions

Chapter 7: Integrating PQC into Existing Systems and Protocols

Think of this chapter as a guide for upgrading the security systems of existing buildings. You can't just tear everything down and start from scratch; you need to carefully integrate new security measures into the existing infrastructure. That requires planning, expertise, and a deep understanding of how the existing systems work. This chapter will cover strategies, tests, and real life examples, for existing systems to be integrated with PQC.

(7.1: PQC in TLS 1.3: Securing Web Communications in the Quantum Age):

Imagine the internet as a vast, interconnected network of roads. TLS 1.3 is the armor plating that protects the vehicles (data packets) traveling along those roads. However, this armor is vulnerable to a new type of weapon: quantum computers. PQC in TLS 1.3 is about upgrading that armor to withstand this new threat.

(The Importance of TLS 1.3):

Before we delve into the specifics of PQC integration, let's emphasize why TLS 1.3 is so important. It's the latest and greatest version of the TLS protocol, offering significant improvements over its predecessors:

- **Improved Security:** TLS 1.3 removes support for many weak and outdated cryptographic algorithms, making it more resistant to attack.
- **Enhanced Performance:** TLS 1.3 streamlines the handshake process, reducing latency and improving the overall performance of web connections.
- **Perfect Forward Secrecy (PFS):** TLS 1.3 mandates the use of PFS, which ensures that even if a server's private key is compromised, past communication cannot be decrypted.

(Why TLS 1.3 Needs PQC:
The problem is, even the best armor is vulnerable to the wrong weapons.

The traditional Public-Key Cryptography can be exploited. We have to update it with PQC.

(The TLS 1.3 Handshake (Revisited):

To understand where PQC comes in, let's refresh our understanding of the TLS 1.3 handshake. It's a series of messages exchanged between the client (e.g., your web browser) and the server (e.g., the website you're visiting) to establish a secure connection:

1. **Client Hello:** The client sends a ClientHello message, advertising the TLS version, supported cipher suites, and extensions.
2. **Server Hello:** The server responds with a ServerHello, selecting the TLS version, cipher suite, and extensions.
3. **Key Exchange:**
4. **Authentication:** Server uses a public-key certificate.
5. **Establishment: Connection.**

(The Vulnerable Points: Key Establishment. We need to make sure that they have all the security features to make the connection.

(How to Integrate PQC into TLS 1.3):

There are two main approaches to integrating PQC into TLS 1.3:

1. **Hybrid Key Exchange:** Combine a traditional key exchange algorithm (like ECDHE) with a PQC algorithm (like CRYSTALS-Kyber). This provides both classical and quantum security. The most common choice is Kyber, which combines with a key exchange to become quantum.

   The goal here is to have both existing and new PQC to secure the encryption!

2. **PQC-Only Key Exchange:** Replace the traditional key exchange algorithm with a PQC algorithm. This provides the strongest level of quantum resistance, but it may not be compatible with older clients and servers that do not support PQC. However, there are still certain risks with only running code from that location.

(The Hybrid Approach: A Cautious and Practical Strategy):

The hybrid approach is generally considered to be the most practical way to integrate PQC into TLS 1.3. It offers a good balance of security and compatibility. In general, it involves a lot of people taking a middle of the road stance with code.

(Practical Challenges and Considerations):

While the hybrid approach is promising, there are still several challenges to overcome:

- **Performance Overhead:** PQC algorithms can be slower than traditional algorithms. Combining them may increase the latency of web connections. It will force some of those speeds to go down.
- **Compatibility Issues:** Integrating PQC requires changes to both client and server software. This can create compatibility issues with older systems that do not support PQC. That is why the code must be able to be adopted for some time.

(The Role of Cipher Suites):

In TLS, cipher suites define the specific cryptographic algorithms that will be used for key exchange, encryption, and authentication. To integrate PQC into TLS 1.3, new cipher suites need to be defined that include PQC algorithms. Here's what to remember about Cypher Suites:

1. Remember there must be an identification of ciphers to be used.
2. The keys, must be of a large enough size, to be used for security.

(Real Python example: Checking Ciphers to look out for vulnerabilities):
We will display sample code,

```python
import ssl

def check_tls_versions_and_ciphers(host, port=443):
    """Checks supported TLS versions and available ciphers
for a given host.

    Args:
        host: The hostname to connect to (string).
        port: The port number (integer, default 443).
    """
    context = ssl.SSLContext(ssl.PROTOCOL_TLS_CLIENT)
```

```
    context.minimum_version = ssl.TLSVersion.TLSv1_2
#Enforcing TLS Version
    try:
        with socket.create_connection((host, port)) as
sock:
            with context.wrap_socket(sock,
server_hostname=host) as ssock:
                print(f"TLS Version: {ssock.version()}")
                print(f"Cipher Suite: {ssock.cipher()}")
    except Exception as e:
        print(f"Error: {e}")

host = "www.google.com"
check_tls_versions_and_ciphers(host)
```

This example runs though the cyphers, which does not implement PQC as part of the structure. So, you must make sure the code is working with this feature.

(Why Check This Code?):
This is an example, and by looking at what we should know, one can implement for PQC, and check if it's working properly.

Personal Perspective: Integrating PQC into TLS 1.3 is a major undertaking. However, it's a necessary step to ensure that web communications remain secure in the quantum age. There's no quick fix, and it takes time and thought to implement.

(What about Implementation?: Unfortunately, existing support for PQC is rare, and will need a code and a method to put the protocols in place. It's best to test this on local servers to see if the system can run.

(In Conclusion):

Integrating PQC into TLS 1.3 is a complex but crucial step toward securing web communications in the quantum age. By carefully evaluating the trade-offs between security, performance, and compatibility, we can ensure that the transition to PQC is smooth and successful.

(7.2: PQC in SSH: Protecting Remote Access from Quantum Attacks):

Imagine SSH as the secure tunnel that allows administrators and developers to access and manage servers remotely. If that tunnel is compromised, attackers can gain complete control of the system. PQC in SSH is about fortifying that tunnel against quantum-powered intrusions.

(Why SSH is a Prime Target):

SSH is a widely used protocol for secure remote access. It's used for a variety of tasks, including:

- System administration: Managing servers, configuring network devices, and performing other administrative tasks.
- File transfer: Securely transferring files between systems.
- Port forwarding: Creating secure tunnels for other applications.

If SSH is compromised, attackers can:

- Gain unauthorized access to sensitive data.
- Install malware.
- Disrupt services.
- Pivot to other systems on the network.

(How SSH Works (Simplified):

Let's simplify how SSH works:

1. **Client Initiation:** You open a terminal window to remote into the host.
2. **Version Exchange:** Negotiate protocol.
3. **Key Exchange:** The client and server negotiate a key with different exchange methods. The cryptography is to ensure the safety of the session.
4. **Authentication:** If keys don't match, the server authenticates the client.
5. **Session established.** The remote device has access!

(The Quantum Vulnerabilities in SSH):

SSH's classical encryption can be broken and accessed through quantum methods. The integrity and connection can be hacked, losing the keys. That is why steps must be taken to ensure that does not happen.

(How to Integrate PQC into SSH):

The IETF is in the process of standardizing PQC algorithms for use in SSH. So, with that we need to create different keys, for the algorithms in place.

- **Adding New Key Exchange Algorithms:** This involves implementing PQC key exchange algorithms and adding them to the list of supported algorithms in SSH clients and servers. OpenSSH has already started to implement some PQC key exchange algorithms as experimental features.
- **Adding New Signature Algorithms:** Digital signatures are used to authenticate the server and the user. PQC signature algorithms can be added to SSH to provide quantum-resistant authentication.
- **Hybrid Key Exchange:** Like TLS.

(Challenges of Integrating PQC into SSH):

Integrating PQC into SSH presents several challenges:

- **Compatibility:** SSH is a widely deployed protocol with many different implementations. Ensuring compatibility between different implementations is a major challenge.
- **Performance:** PQC algorithms can be slower than traditional algorithms, potentially impacting the performance of SSH connections. It also creates overhead.
- **Standards:** New standards are needed to.

(Code Examples for Integration: Unfortunately, there is no python for direct integration, however we will look into the code that would happen with this. In this case, we want to display code for the following process,

1. The code will use PQC code, to connect to the server.
2. Key rotation (for security in case of code break).
3. Multi Factor Authentication.

(It can also provide access to the command code, or more.)

(Best practices to secure SSH access):

It is highly important to secure keys for access. It should be made a highly secured point of access in any network, be it a cloud, or a company device. The most important is protection of keys, in order to ensure security.

In addition, code review, regular patching, and testing of the code are also important for the overall security. Always remember, if there is a hole in the code, and you do not see it, a bad actor will.

(How to Perform Code and Protocol Review:
*Testing must be done at regular points, to ensure safety.
*Code must be from known sources.
*Make sure keys are not compromised!

(Conclusion):

Securing SSH with PQC is a crucial step towards protecting our systems and data from quantum attacks. By staying informed, prioritizing security, and adopting a layered approach, we can ensure that our remote access remains secure in the quantum age. It protects all the access to our internal devices and cloud from attacks. This ensures for better, safe and secure code.

(7.3: PQC for VPNs, Messaging Apps, and Other Security Protocols):

Imagine PQC as a shield that can be deployed around different areas.

(VPNs (Virtual Private Networks): Securing Network Traffic:

VPNs create secure, encrypted connections over a public network, typically the internet. They're used to protect your online activity from eavesdropping, especially on public Wi-Fi networks. They secure what can be seen on the web, so that your data can be safe.

(VPN Protocols and Their Vulnerabilities):

VPNs rely on various protocols to establish and maintain secure connections, including:

- **IPsec (Internet Protocol Security):** A suite of protocols that provides secure communication at the IP layer. It's commonly used in site-to-site VPNs and supports both transport mode (encrypting the payload of IP packets) and tunnel mode (encrypting the entire IP packet).
- **OpenVPN:** An open-source VPN protocol that uses TLS/SSL for key exchange and encryption. It's highly configurable and supports a wide range of cryptographic algorithms.
- **WireGuard:** A relatively new VPN protocol that emphasizes simplicity and performance. It uses state-of-the-art cryptography and is designed to be easy to deploy and configure.

Like TLS and SSH, these protocols rely on classic cryptography which again, puts them at a high security risk. It then creates different issues that will need to be evaluated for the upcoming transfer to the quantum area.

(Adding PQC Code):
All areas will need these PQC in particular; The process will look something like this,
1). Add authentication.
2). Add encryption.
3). Replace the hash mode with quantum-resistant HASH functions.

(Messaging Apps: Protecting Private Communications):

Messaging apps have become an essential part of modern communication, allowing us to exchange text, images, audio, and video with friends, family, and colleagues. Security is very important in this sector.

(End-to-End Encryption (E2EE):

To protect the privacy of our conversations, many messaging apps use end-to-end encryption (E2EE). With E2EE, messages are encrypted on the sender's device and can only be decrypted on the recipient's device. This prevents the messaging app provider (or any eavesdropper) from reading the messages.

Several popular messaging apps use E2EE, including:

- Signal
- WhatsApp

- Telegram

(The Challenges of PQC in Messaging Apps):

Integrating PQC into messaging apps presents some unique challenges:

- **Performance:** Messaging apps need to be responsive and efficient, even on low-powered devices. PQC algorithms should not significantly impact performance.
- **Key Distribution:** Managing and distributing PQC keys securely can be complex, especially in large groups.
- **Perfect Forward Secrecy (PFS)** This will allow people to make sure the new code is safe.

(Other Security Protocols):

PQC is relevant to other security protocols as well, including:

- **S/MIME (Secure/Multipurpose Internet Mail Extensions):** A standard for encrypting and digitally signing email messages.
- **DNSSEC (Domain Name System Security Extensions):** A suite of protocols that provides authentication and integrity for DNS data.
- **Kerberos:** A network authentication protocol used to verify the identity of users and services.

(Analogy: Public Water Treatment):
If we were to look at a town, there are many ways for water to come in and out. The same code can be seen with cryptography for the internet, where there are multiple ports of access. There must be a level of trust and security of cryptography.

(Implementation in Action (Though Cannot be Done Directly):
This is a simulation, to show how something can be checked,

1. The python code will check for vulnerability for certain files.
2. Follow well known authentication to check if the key is well followed.
3. To add the signature, create a good code.

(Why are all those points important?):
While we can not perform each of these in the real world, if there was a system in place that could do this, these steps would be an excellent approach.

(Best Code Safety: Keep The Code On Lockdown):

The use of public and private keys needs to be followed with strict guidelines, so keys do not get lost or stolen. The same can be said with protocols for use and security!

(Conclusion):

Extending PQC protections to VPNs, messaging apps, and other security protocols is essential for creating a truly quantum-resistant digital ecosystem. The key is to approach PQC implementation holistically across your technology stack and to make security more diversified. A multi code approach!

(7.4: Coexistence Strategies: Hybrid Approaches for a Gradual Transition):

Imagine upgrading a jet engine mid-flight. You can't just rip out the old engine and install the new one; you need a carefully planned transition that ensures the plane keeps flying safely. Similarly, we need to develop coexistence strategies that allow us to gradually migrate to PQC without disrupting our existing systems and protocols. This can be achieved through hybrid systems, and other means to provide a gradual transitions

(The Need for a Gradual Transition):

A "flag day" approach – where everyone switches to PQC at the same time – is simply not feasible. The internet is a complex, interconnected system with millions of devices and applications. Coordinating a simultaneous upgrade would be a logistical nightmare. Instead, a transition must gradually happen.

A big threat to PQC is, the unknown. Because new systems have to be created, the risk of compromise can be a security threat in itself, that also needs to be secured.

(What will need to happen to ensure a gradual transition?):

A gradual integration will need the following to be implemented and used,

1). Code must be able to talk to old code.

2). The hardware must be able to work with older system and new ones.

3). All users of the code, be it companies, individuals, etc, must be able to smoothly and correctly implement the product.

(Common Coexistence Strategies:

Let's explore some common coexistence strategies that can be used to gradually transition to PQC:

1. **Hybrid Key Exchange:** Combine a traditional key exchange algorithm (e.g., ECDHE) with a PQC algorithm (e.g., CRYSTALS-Kyber). This provides both classical and quantum security. Here you can implement a parallel system for the code.
2. **Algorithm Agility:** Design systems that can easily switch between different cryptographic algorithms. This allows you to quickly adopt new PQC algorithms as they become available and to respond to any security vulnerabilities that are discovered. If the code works, or has trouble, you can use the different options.
3. **Dual Signatures:** Use both a traditional signature (e.g., RSA) and a PQC signature (e.g., CRYSTALS-Dilithium) to sign documents or code. This allows older systems to verify the traditional signature while newer systems can verify the PQC signature. This provides backward compatibility while also preparing for the quantum future. If one works, the other can be reviewed.
4. **Tunneling/Encapsulation** Encapsulating all the traffic and data through a PQC system makes it secure without directly impacting code!
5. **Migration Planning**: Create migration plans that are secure. To reduce the chance of cyber threats, always test new systems before they are launched.

(The Importance of Risk Assessment:
The key is, to understand the risks in cyber and quantum world and to code around those problems. Assess and look out for what can be done!

(Code: What Does This Look Like?):

Let's create a code to show security, as more security is always a high point to improve the system!

```python
    import os
from cryptography.fernet import Fernet
from cryptography.hazmat.primitives import hashes
from cryptography.hazmat.primitives.kdf.pbkdf2 import
PBKDF2HMAC
from cryptography.hazmat.backends import default_backend
from cryptography.exceptions import InvalidTag

def generate_key_from_password(password, salt):
    """Generates a Fernet key from a password using
PBKDF2."""
    password_bytes = password.encode('utf-8')
    salt_bytes = salt  #Salt should be in bytes

    kdf = PBKDF2HMAC(
        algorithm=hashes.SHA256(),
        length=32,  #Fernet key size is 32 bytes
        salt=salt_bytes,
        iterations=100000, #Recommended number of
iterations
        backend=default_backend()
    )
    key = kdf.derive(password_bytes)
    return key

def encrypt_data(data, key):
    """Encrypts data using Fernet with a provided key."""
    f = Fernet(key)
    encrypted_data = f.encrypt(data.encode('utf-8'))
    return encrypted_data

def decrypt_data(encrypted_data, key):
    """Decrypts data using Fernet with a provided key."""
    f = Fernet(key)
    try:
        decrypted_data =
f.decrypt(encrypted_data).decode('utf-8')
        return decrypted_data
    except InvalidTag:
        return None #Authentication failed

def main():
    # 1. Password based Key Derivation
    password = input("Enter your password: ")
```

113

```
    salt = os.urandom(16) #Generate a new random salt for
each key
    key = generate_key_from_password(password, salt)

    # 2. Encryption
    data = "Sensitive information to protect."
    encrypted_data = encrypt_data(data, key)
    print(f"Encrypted data: {encrypted_data}")

    # 3. Decryption
    decrypted_data = decrypt_data(encrypted_data, key)

    if decrypted_data:
        print(f"Decrypted data: {decrypted_data}")
    else:
        print("Decryption failed (likely incorrect
password).")
```

Security Warning: Remember that the security depends heavily on password strength

(In Summary):

Always rotate your keys, use diversified key sources, have multi level authentication, and test what you put out. If you do this, your PQC code will work.

(Code from Python, is good and should be noted for safety.)

(Best Practices for a Gradual Transition):

In any change to something new, keep a review, and make sure the proper tests are made. The same can be said with anything in PQC security. A bad move, can be costly.

Personal Perspective: The transition to PQC will be a marathon, not a sprint. It will require sustained effort, collaboration, and a willingness to adapt to new challenges.

(Concluding thoughts)

The gradual transition will need all parties to be on board. Once everyone can do their best and plan, the transition to more secured data can be on the way, to help the security of us all. Take a great risk assessment and move on from there!

Chapter 8: Practical Considerations for PQC Implementation

Imagine you're building a house. You have the blueprints and the materials, but you also need to consider practical things like the plumbing, electrical wiring, and insulation. Similarly, implementing PQC requires attention to details beyond just the cryptographic algorithms themselves. It includes hardware, data migration, and maintenance plans.

(8.1: Hardware Acceleration and Software Optimization Techniques):

Imagine you're a race car engineer. You've got a powerful engine (the PQC algorithm), but you also need to optimize the aerodynamics, suspension, and tires to squeeze every last bit of performance out of the car. Similarly, hardware acceleration and software optimization are about fine-tuning the entire system to maximize the performance of PQC.

(The Need for Speed):

Why is performance so important? While it is vital for a security to take place, slow systems also present challenges. A common exploit that people can take advantage of, is the use of too much energy.

The Two Main Approaches:

The techniques can be categorized:

1. *Hardware-Acceleration*: Using specialized hardware (like GPUs or FPGAs) to speed up the core cryptographic operations. This involves a change, and more time to work.
2. *Software Optimization*: Code improvements on a system, to provide more output with a more secured result.

Hardware Acceleration: Unleashing the Power of Specialized Hardware:

Hardware acceleration involves offloading computationally intensive tasks from the CPU to specialized hardware devices that are designed to perform those tasks more efficiently. This can significantly improve the performance of PQC algorithms.

Some types are,

1. *Dedicated Crypto Accelerators:* Certain processors come with them. This allows speed for the operations.
2. *GPUs (Graphics Processing Units):* The use of different and multiple parallel processors allow power to be generated over large amounts of data to be computed. The GPUs, provide greater memory for processing.
3. *FPGAs (Field-Programmable Gate Arrays):* Reconfigurable hardware devices allow for different and complex code for every step.

(When to Consider Hardware Acceleration):

- **High-Throughput Applications:** Hardware acceleration is particularly beneficial for applications that require high throughput, such as web servers, VPN gateways, and network appliances. This improves how people access data on a regular basis.
- **Low-Latency Applications:** It can also improve the speed it takes to compute the data.
- **Resource-Constrained Devices:** On embedded systems with limited CPU power, offloading cryptographic operations to dedicated hardware can free up resources and improve overall system performance. This will allow those with low powered systems to improve access and security for their code.

(Software Optimization Techniques: Fine-Tuning the Code):

Software optimization techniques are used to improve the efficiency of the code itself. This involves reducing the number of instructions that need to be executed, minimizing memory accesses, and taking advantage of the specific features of the target platform. This code optimization, is a cheaper way to go than that of a hardware implementation.

(Code Example: Optimized System over Another:
The goal in this part, is to create a faster time to check hash code.
The code is as follows,

```
      import hashlib
import time

def hash_data_optimized(algorithm, data):
    """Hashes data using the selected algorithm and
measures the runtime.
    The code is optimized for efficiency.

    Args:
        algorithm: hash function.
        data: the data to hash, in bytes.

    Return:
        A tuple: (hash value, time taken for the process).
    """
    start = time.perf_counter()
    hashed_data = algorithm(data).hexdigest()
    end = time.perf_counter()

    return hashed_data, end - start

def hash_data_less_optimized(algorithm, data):
  """Hashes the input data using the specified algorithm
and measures performance.
  The code is designed for readability, not peak
efficiency.

  Args:
      algorithm: The hashlib algorithm (e.g.,
hashlib.sha256).
      data: The data to hash (bytes).

  Returns:
      A tuple containing the hash value and the time taken.
  """
  start_time = time.time()
  algorithm(data).hexdigest()
  end_time = time.time()
  elapsed_time = end_time - start_time
  return algorithm(data).hexdigest(), elapsed_time

#Example data:
data = b"This is data that needs to be hashed. " * 10000

#Test
```

```
hash_SHA, opt = hash_data_optimized(hashlib.sha256, data)
hash_SHA_less , less_opt =
hash_data_less_optimized(hashlib.sha256, data)

print (opt)
print (less_opt)
```

(Analysis of the Code):

1. Reduced Code Size: If lines are small, the less time it will take to compute.
2. Data Types: Small code is more memory efficient and will make it easier to complete an algorithm.

(In Conclusion):
Combining hardware acceleration with careful software optimization is essential for achieving acceptable performance with PQC algorithms. By selecting the right tools and techniques for the job, you can ensure that your PQC implementations are both secure and efficient.

(This is a highly technical feat to do, you will need to consult with someone who knows a lot about coding.)

(8.2: Key Management in the Post-Quantum World: Generation, Storage, and Distribution):

Imagine your cryptographic keys as the master keys to your entire digital kingdom. If those keys fall into the wrong hands, the entire kingdom is vulnerable. Key management is about creating a system for generating, storing, distributing, and destroying those keys in a way that minimizes the risk of compromise. If the key is compromised, the kingdom does not exist.

(The Key Management Lifecycle):

Key management is not a one-time event; it's an ongoing process that encompasses the entire lifecycle of a cryptographic key:

1. **Generation:** How are the keys created? Are they generated using a cryptographically secure random number generator?

2. **Storage:** Where are the keys stored? Are they protected from unauthorized access?
3. **Distribution:** How are the keys distributed to authorized users and systems? Are they protected during transit?
4. **Usage:** How are the keys used to encrypt and decrypt data or sign and verify messages? Are they used in a secure manner?
5. **Revocation:** What happens when a key is compromised or no longer needed? How is it revoked or destroyed?

(Challenges in the Post-Quantum World):

The transition to PQC introduces new challenges for key management:

- **Larger Key Sizes:** PQC algorithms often have larger key sizes than traditional algorithms. This can make key storage and distribution more complex. The bigger the data, the more room there is for error.
- **New Attack Vectors:** Quantum computers may be able to break existing key exchange protocols, making it necessary to develop new key exchange mechanisms that are resistant to quantum attacks. With greater power, comes more power for attacks!
- **Long-Term Security:** How do we ensure that our PQC keys remain secure for decades to come, even as quantum computers continue to develop? The long term security is that you have new and multiple checks for security with data encryption.

(Key Generation: Ensuring Strong and Unpredictable Keys):

Key generation is the foundation of any cryptographic system. If the keys are weak or predictable, the entire system is vulnerable. Therefore, the keys must be strong.

(Best Practices for Key Generation):

- **Use a Cryptographically Secure Random Number Generator (CSPRNG):** Always use a CSPRNG to generate cryptographic keys. CSPRNGs are designed to produce random numbers that are unpredictable and suitable for cryptographic applications. They often use entropy from the environment to make them more secured.

- **Seed the CSPRNG Properly:** The CSPRNG must be seeded with a sufficient amount of entropy. Entropy is a measure of randomness. The more entropy, the more unpredictable the random numbers will be.

Personal Perspective: I've seen too many systems that use weak or predictable random number generators. It's a recipe for disaster. Always use a CSPRNG and make sure it's properly seeded!

(Key Storage: Protecting Keys from Unauthorized Access):

Once the keys have been generated, it's essential to protect them from unauthorized access. If an attacker gains access to your keys, they can decrypt your data, forge your signatures, and impersonate you. Therefore, storage must be important.

(Best Practices for Key Storage):

- **Hardware Security Modules (HSMs):** HSMs are dedicated hardware devices that are designed to securely store and manage cryptographic keys. They provide a high level of physical and logical security and are often used in high-security environments. They are more code and security.
- **Key Management Systems (KMS):** KMSs are software systems that provide a centralized way to manage cryptographic keys. KMSs can help to automate key rotation, enforce access control policies, and provide auditing and logging capabilities. They also offer more tools and code.
- **Encryption at Rest:** Always encrypt your keys when they are stored on disk. This provides an additional layer of protection in case the storage device is compromised.
- **Access Control:** Implement strict access control policies to limit who can access the keys. Only authorized users and systems should be able to access the keys, only and if they are needed.
- **Regular Audits:** Conduct regular audits of your key storage systems to ensure that they are secure. Testing with keys, and seeing how the storage and access is to be looked out for is vital.

(Key Distribution: Securely Delivering Keys to Authorized Parties):

Key distribution is the process of securely delivering cryptographic keys to authorized users and systems. This can be a challenging task, especially in distributed environments. They must not be intercepted by bad actors who would abuse access.

(Code Testing):
It is difficult to review in code form, however, a system to test for the following, is something that should be kept in mind.

1. The tests will need to generate encryption of keys.
2. Keys only available to right people.
3. Check for old code in key management system, replace if need be.
4. Log all code changes and new versions of key code.

(In Conclusion):

Key management is a critical aspect of any cryptographic system, and it's especially important in the post-quantum world. PQC algorithms often have larger sizes, and need to have security.

(8.3: Testing and Validation: Ensuring the Security and Correctness of PQC Implementations):

Imagine building a skyscraper. You wouldn't just trust the blueprints and the construction crew; you'd subject the building to rigorous inspections and stress tests to ensure it can withstand earthquakes, wind, and other real-world conditions. Similarly, testing and validation are about putting your PQC implementations through their paces to identify any weaknesses or vulnerabilities. PQC, is not much different than trying to erect new, complex structures that are not meant to bend in the wind!

(The Importance of Rigorous Testing):

Why is rigorous testing so important for PQC implementations?
It's important to make sure new codes work and are safe, as they are made available. If new code that has not been tested or been subject to safety checks, then a compromise can occur and data will be hacked. You must remember that code is good, but if done badly, code can be disastrous!

(What is it Important to Test?):

1. **To test for safety.**
2. **The coding must be correct.**
3. **The system must be stable.**
4. **To make sure that it does what its intent is.**

(Types of Testing):
You need both to ensure that the final product is secure and robust.
There are tests to perform to find these key answers:

1. *Functional testing*: You put something to see if there are any security issues, if the file can run, or if the code delivers to a device, it will be put to the test. Testing has a lot to to with what was previously stated.
2. *Test for security*: Try and break in. Can the software be hacked.

(Validation Code: Is The Code Working?):

If there is no code that has been put in to action, then we can not see what is working. How do you test to see if it has been corrupted?

(There are also ways for code, to run, not to have problems)

(What To Look Out For:)

1. It is highly recommended to perform black box testing! This is the most efficient and secure path to test code.
2. Code must also be from a trustworthy source.

Personal Perspective: Testing is often seen as a necessary evil, but I see it as an opportunity to learn more about the system and to identify potential problems before they become real-world disasters. It's a chance to put on your "attacker" hat and try to break the system in every way imaginable. You must look into all angles to prevent security.

(The Need to Follow Testing):
If all the testings go as they should, they should be applied for security! After that, it can be looked to for security.

(Testing to See If all Works out):
Let's look for safety, by using old files, and testing it with new.

If a problem is found, that new code is not secure, or that there will be an issue to continue.

It can be as simple as testing to see if you can log in or out.

(Key Aspects of a Testing Plan

1. Testing and safety first!
2. Regular testing to prevent exploits is key!
3. A solid plan on how the code will be checked.

(Conclusion):

By seeing and working through the many ideas and concepts, one can code through the coming quantum period. Make sure and review the safety, to continue in a secure system!

Chapter 9: Migration Strategies: A Step-by-Step Guide to Quantum Readiness

Imagine you're moving a city. You can't just pick everything up and move it overnight; you need a phased approach that considers infrastructure, transportation, housing, and the needs of the citizens. Similarly, migrating to PQC requires careful planning and a phased approach to ensure a smooth transition. Moving to PQC requires, knowing the risk, budget, plan, and employee training.

(The Urgency of Planning):

Before we get into the specifics, let's reiterate why planning for PQC migration is so important *now*, even if quantum computers aren't an immediate threat:
With that being said, preparation is KEY!

(9.1: Risk Assessment: Identifying Vulnerable Data and Systems):

Imagine you're a general tasked with defending a city. You wouldn't just spread your troops randomly; you'd identify the most strategic locations (power plants, communication hubs, etc.) and concentrate your defenses there. Similarly, a PQC risk assessment involves pinpointing the most critical data and systems that need quantum-resistant protection.

(Why is a Risk Assessment So Important?):

A thorough risk assessment is essential for several reasons:

- **Prioritization:** It helps you prioritize your PQC migration efforts, focusing on the most critical assets first.
- **Resource Allocation:** It informs decisions about how to allocate resources (time, money, personnel) to protect different systems and data.

- **Informed Decision-Making:** A well-conducted risk assessment provides a clear picture of the organization's overall security posture and informs decisions about which PQC algorithms and implementation strategies are most appropriate.

(The Key Steps in a PQC Risk Assessment):

Let's break down the process into manageable steps:

1. **Identify Critical Assets:** The first step is to identify the data and systems that are most critical to your organization. These are the assets that would have the greatest impact on your business if they were compromised by a quantum attack.
   - **Consider What is important for you**: Data that is extremely classified, private, and worth it to encrypt should always be focused on first.

What systems are there to see what to secure? Make sure that the more important systems are worked on first to be more secure.
This is an ongoing process and needs to be checked at all times.

1. **Identify Cryptographic Dependencies:** Once you've identified your critical assets, the next step is to identify the cryptographic algorithms that are used to protect them. This involves inventorying all the systems, applications, and protocols that rely on cryptography.

The way for encryption is that you must keep those code safe, by having limited access.

1. **Assess Threats and Vulnerabilities:** The next step is to assess the threats and vulnerabilities that could compromise your critical assets.
   This can involve using code that is known, with many checks.
2. **Determine Risk Levels:** Determine the level of risk associated with each asset. This involves considering the likelihood of a successful attack and the potential impact of the attack. Make sure that all the keys can be changed or rotated in case there are any security threats in the coding!
3. **Create Action**: What do you want to do with the information? This is how the most secure systems and data are protected.

(What to Evaluate) What systems need a better test? Test for different things to create more safe and secure measures.

(Creating The Steps):

There will need to be a system made for a test. All must always be evaluated.
*List for every code, is there an exploit.

*Make checks, with different passwords, to see how it protects from attacks.

- If all code and information to protect is set, then it will be ready for launch.

(Make sure it works, test it on local to review the final code)

(What to Always Check and Know)
Test as much code and versions, to be ready for possible attacks.
Know the most used codes, their uses, benefits, and if they might be easy to hack, because they are commonly known! It's about how to better secure yourself.

(A High Level Example With Python Code Showing File Search and Information):
The code, will just be here to present how one could access some data for a search, to look for a password. This is used only to help the process of information gathering.

NOTE: Do not put your data or password here, just follow and learn concepts and tips:

```
    import os
import re
import hashlib

def search_files_for_passwords(root_dir,
password_patterns):
    """Searches files in a directory for potential
passwords using regex patterns.

    Args:
```

```python
        root_dir: The root directory to start the search
from (string).
        password_patterns: A list of regex patterns to
search for (list of strings).

    Returns:
        A dictionary where keys are filenames and values
are lists of matching lines.
    """
    results = {}
    for dirpath, dirnames, filenames in os.walk(root_dir):
        for filename in filenames:
            filepath = os.path.join(dirpath, filename)
            try:
                with open(filepath, 'r', encoding='utf-8')
as f:  # Handle character encoding
                    for i, line in enumerate(f):
                        for pattern in password_patterns:
                            if re.search(pattern, line):
                                if filepath not in results:
                                    results[filepath] = []

results[filepath].append(f"{i+1}: {line.strip()}") #Record
the line number

            except Exception as e: #Handles
                print(f"Could not process {filepath}: {e}")
#Error display
    return results

def hash_file(filepath):
    """Calculates the SHA-256 hash of a file.

    Args:
        filepath: The path to the file (string).

    Returns:
        The SHA-256 hash of the file (string).
    """
    hasher = hashlib.sha256()
    try:
        with open(filepath, 'rb') as afile:
            buf = afile.read()
            hasher.update(buf)
        return hasher.hexdigest()
    except Exception as e:
        print(f"Error hashing {filepath}: {e}")
        return None
```

```python
def identify_crypto_usage(root_dir,
interesting_extensions=(".py", ".java", ".c", ".cpp")):
    """Identifies potential usage of cryptography in source
code files based on extensions and content.

    Args:
        root_dir: The root directory to start the search
from (string).
        interesting_extensions: A tuple of file extensions
to consider (tuple of strings).

    Returns:
        A dictionary where keys are filenames and values
are lists of "hits".
    """

    results = {}
    crypto_keywords = ["cryptography", "ssl", "tls", "aes",
"rsa", "des", "hashlib", "jwt", "openssl", "bcrypt",
"scrypt"]

    for dirpath, dirnames, filenames in os.walk(root_dir):
        for filename in filenames:
            if filename.endswith(interesting_extensions):
                filepath = os.path.join(dirpath, filename)
                try:
                    with open(filepath, 'r', encoding='utf-
8') as f:
                        for i, line in enumerate(f):
                            lower_line = line.lower()
                            for keyword in crypto_keywords:
                                if keyword in lower_line:
                                    if filepath not in
results:
                                        results[filepath] =
[]

results[filepath].append(f"{i+1}: {line.strip()}")
                except Exception as e:
                    print(f"Could not process {filepath}:
{e}")
    return results
```

"A journey of a thousand miles begins with a single step." The first step towards quantum readiness is to perform a thorough risk assessment to identify your organization's most vulnerable data and systems. So, start planning today! Remember that, security, is the goal!
Thank you.

(9.2: Developing a PQC Migration Plan: Prioritization, Resource Allocation, and Timelines):

Think of this as creating a detailed construction schedule for building a new, quantum-resistant wing onto your existing data center. You need to prioritize the most critical areas, allocate resources effectively, and set realistic timelines to ensure the project is completed on time and within budget. A plan is like a blueprint that everyone can follow, to make sure everything is safe and correct.

(The Importance of a Well-Defined Migration Plan):

A well-defined PQC migration plan is essential for several reasons:

- **Coordination:** It provides a framework for coordinating the efforts of different teams and departments within your organization. All must be known.
- **Prioritization:** What to put first?
- **Resource Management:** Money, people, time, and action must all match correctly.
- **Risk Mitigation:** The goal of the system is for the protection of the overall network, and what action can prevent it from happening?
- **Progress Tracking:** If there is a method in place, then you can see if goals are being met.

(Key Elements of a PQC Migration Plan):

Let's break down the key elements that should be included in your PQC migration plan:

1. **Prioritization:** This involves ranking your critical assets based on their vulnerability to quantum attacks and the potential impact of a compromise.

Which key aspects need to have extra protection? All steps are to be followed as much as possible, for them all to be secured to all.
You should do a code audit, to understand what the system does.

1. **Cryptography Inventory and Modernization:** You need to create and update the list in order to have a better understanding. Modernized codes, better code are a good start.

What cryptography code works?

It's also very important to plan for rotation of codes, in order to prevent people to keep up to date, and to prevent future hacks!

1. **Resource Allocation:** How to handle it all? Resources for your PQC migration include:
   *Money: What budget to stay in.
   *Staff: What staff need to be kept and known.
   *Consultations: You must talk to experts!

- New Tools: Update often to stay on top.

How will you use those tools?
It needs to happen smoothly.

1. **Define timelines**. Key timeline parts will be,

- Code testing and planning (6 months)
- Test Implementation (9 Months)
- Final and code review (10 Months)

It needs to happen in a logical order to prevent problems.

(Why Does Implementation Occur First Before a Final Code)
The first step is the goal of PQC and how it protects! With that security, it will all come together.

(6. Employee Training for Better Protection):

Even with a detailed plan, success relies on people with the needed knowledge. With no training, there is an opening for problems to come into play.

Personal Perspective: I've seen many well-intentioned projects fail because of a lack of training and awareness among employees. Make sure your employees understand the importance of PQC and how to implement it correctly! It always relies on who knows the system and what is going on!

(Code Demonstration (Planning and Implementation)*
Because there is no true, perfect code, it will need to be secured with the right method. The python example, is an excellent way to look for different potential points. It can be used to search for key terms. This provides a basis for something real!

```python
    import os
import re
import hashlib

def search_files_for_patterns(root_dir, patterns):
    """Searches files in a directory for specified regex
patterns.

    Args:
        root_dir: The root directory to start the search
from (string).
        patterns: A list of regex patterns to search for
(list of strings).

    Returns:
        A dictionary where keys are filenames and values
are lists of matching lines.
    """
    results = {}
    for dirpath, dirnames, filenames in os.walk(root_dir):
        for filename in filenames:
            filepath = os.path.join(dirpath, filename)
            try:
                with open(filepath, 'r', encoding='utf-8')
as f: #Encoding with files that can be encoded
                    for i, line in enumerate(f): #Line and
loop
                        for pattern in patterns:
                            if re.search(pattern, line):
                                if filepath not in results:
#The path to not get the results
                                    results[filepath] = []

results[filepath].append(f"{i+1}: {line.strip()}") #Strip
and take note, of the loop back!
            except Exception as e: # if something goes
wrong, you have to use an encoding that does not compute.
                print(f"Could not process {filepath}: {e}")
    return results
```

```python
def create_report(search_results,
output_file="pqc_migration_report.txt"):
    """Creates a report summarizing the search results.

    Args:
        search_results: A dictionary of search results
(from search_files_for_patterns).
        output_file: The name of the output file (string).
    """
    with open(output_file, 'w', encoding='utf-8') as
outfile:
        outfile.write("PQC Migration Planning Report\n")
        outfile.write("-----------------------------\n\n")

        if not search_results:
            outfile.write("No potential cryptographic
usages found.\n")
        else:
            for filepath, matches in
search_results.items():
                outfile.write(f"File: {filepath}\n")
                for match in matches:
                    outfile.write(f"\t{match}\n")
                outfile.write("\n")
        print(f"Report saved to {output_file}")

# Example Usage
root_directory = "." # Search from this location
search_patterns = [
    r"cryptography",  #Check for "cryptography"
    r"ssl\.wrap_socket", #SSL wrapping
    r"hashlib\.sha256",   #Check hashing algorithms
    r"Fernet\(",  #Check use of Fernet encryption
    r"from cryptography", #Check if the crytography package
used.
    r"subprocess\.run" #Look for shell
]

results = search_files_for_patterns(root_directory,
search_patterns)
create_report(results) #Creates report!

# --- Add analysis of results to guide action.
```

(In Summary):

The key is, what to test, and that all key components must have key actions. With those action, that makes it all the more easier to put data in place. What the goal of what needs to be seen.

(9.3: Vendor Selection: Evaluating PQC-Ready Products and Services):

Think of this as choosing a construction company to build that new, quantum-resistant wing onto your data center. You wouldn't just hire the first company that comes along; you'd carefully evaluate their experience, expertise, security practices, and ability to deliver a high-quality product.

(The Importance of Due Diligence:
It will be difficult to find one that is the right pick, but it's a good system to follow in any situation. Follow those ideas in all circumstances.

(Key Steps in the Vendor Selection Process:
Here is that guide:

*Identify Business Demands.
*Identify potential providers.
*Check each vendor through those questions.
*Score all the tests.

Weigh the pros and the cons, to make sure you find who the right code and vendor must have! If no good, or to many errors, it's time to pull the plug.

Personal Perspective: I've seen too many organizations get burned by vendors who overpromise and underdeliver, or who have questionable security practices. Taking the time to thoroughly evaluate vendors upfront can save you a lot of headaches down the road.

(What To Look For):

Make sure they know what there are doing. Check there website, see if there any known violations, and make sure they have been working in the location.

How can we help prevent that for your future security?

- **Security and Reliability:**. Is that data secured? Do people say it secure? What is the guarantee.
- **Follow those steps to build an ideal product.**
- Follow all code

1. Review The Code: If the code is all original, and there is a copy, there will be legal problems on the way for its implementation.
2. Implementation and Data is Known: If the data and test show that the code functions, you can know that it can be put to great use! Test code from multiple places to make sure there are more safety protocols to follow.

(What else can you find? Code must be stable, or can be a security risk. Code and security go hand and hand.

1. *Does the Team Have a Reputable Name?*

If no one knows who the product came from, or if there are more, then there can not be trust. In many cases, having and knowing their name, as a source, can help with it's review. There should be a contact if there is a breach.

1. *Can I Check on what Was Done?*

You are not alone, ask other security experts! By working with those people, there is a greater chance that more of this becomes a secured format that will prevent attacks. Use what knowledge you have! If you have the knowledge, then go for what seems and feels right. You need to have faith as all else is tested.

(Remember There Must Be A Review.)

What can be a big test? Test data! You will then be ready for the quantum world!

(Best Practices to Keep the Momentum!):

1. Use people to talk to.
2. Always remember that all code can be hacked.
3. Plan for everything!

(Final Words)

The key, is test. Make code with multiple reviews, plan, see and learn from any mistakes. It is how you see a system works.
It has been a gift to help, thank you!

(9.4: Employee Training: Building Internal Expertise in Quantum-Safe Security):

Imagine building a state-of-the-art hospital with the latest equipment. It would be useless without trained doctors, nurses, and technicians to operate the equipment and provide patient care. Similarly, even the best PQC algorithms and systems are ineffective without trained employees who understand how to use them.

(The Human Element in Cybersecurity):

Cybersecurity is not just about technology; it's also about people. Employees are often the first line of defense against cyberattacks, and they need to be trained to recognize and respond to threats. This is one of the first things you need to do.

(How to Teach About The Human Element):

1. Find the important people.
2. Create and test different security codes.
3. Test and review how to secure data.

These action plans, are just some, of the methods to create more awareness.

(You Will Need To Test: Is There Vulnerability?):

- They know everything to keep in mind and review.
- The correct actions.

(Key Training Topics for Quantum-Safe Security):

- *What is A quantum Computer?* So all people can know code protection, everyone must understand how to protect and understand the attack.
- *Cryptography Background:*. This is one of the big starting points. You must know and review code history to be better.
- *Key Points of security with passwords*: Every password can be a tool for a hacker. The steps for password management are key for everyone to understand.

(The Importance of Role-Based Training):

Not all employees need the same level of training. The training should be tailored to the specific roles and responsibilities of each employee.

- *Security Engineers*: The most important job is to train those.
- *Other Tech People: There must be an awareness.*
  *General: All employees should be told key things, to prevent any exploits from happening.

(Creating The Program):

- The course should cover it all.
- It needs to have clear goals.
- Tests and quizzes at the end.

Personal Perspective: I've seen firsthand the positive impact of well-designed security awareness training programs. Employees who are educated about security threats are more likely to make smart decisions and avoid falling victim to attacks. I have even been trained and feel that the right information is key!

Part IV: The Future of Cybersecurity in the Quantum Age

Chapter 10: Challenges and Open Questions in Post-Quantum Cryptography

Think of this as assessing the long-term weather forecast after building a city's flood defenses. You've prepared for the known risks, but you also need to consider potential future threats and adapt your defenses accordingly. PQC is not a static field; it's constantly evolving.

(10.1: Long-Term Security: The Threat of New Quantum Algorithms):

Imagine building a fortress. You might design it to withstand the best siege weapons of today, but what if a new, more powerful weapon is invented tomorrow? You need to be prepared to adapt your defenses to meet the evolving threat. We need to prepare for the known, and more importantly, unknown.

(The Limitations of Current Security Proofs):

Many PQC algorithms come with security proofs, which provide mathematical evidence that the algorithm is resistant to certain types of attacks. However, these proofs are often based on assumptions about the hardness of certain mathematical problems, and there's always a possibility that these assumptions will turn out to be false.
Most of this, is that the assumption that one set of algorithms are all that is present.

(The Importance of Constant Vigilance):

The breaking of SIKE serves as a reminder that even algorithms that have been subjected to years of scrutiny can still have hidden weaknesses. We must always be on the lookout for new attack techniques.

(Code, If Broken, Can Get You In Trouble):

There are a few real problems when code and security has been violated:
*Compromised code.
*If the code can be traced to you, there can be lawsuits!
*Loss of Data.

Make sure to code with extreme safety, or all can come crashing down.
All data that is being lost will have many negative problems.

(Why Is There Always Going to Be Security Issues?:

- **Algorithmic Diversity and Dependence:**

Algorithms always have dependencies, and in a lot of ways, new exploits will be based on old code being tested and taken apart.

The key is to test and fix problems before that happens! This is a big game of cat and mouse.

- **What new codes come out?**
  As the new algorithms are formed, those need to be re-evaluated to the most up-to date code that has also taken the test to see if it is all up to snuff.

Personal Perspective: I've learned that in cybersecurity, complacency is the enemy. You can never assume that your systems are perfectly secure. You always need to be looking for new threats and vulnerabilities.

(Code Check - What Would we do):

There is nothing we can put to display the PQC nature of the code. However, this will highlight that we must put our minds to. What is important about python code is that the testing of the software, and how it can be prevented:

1). Code checks, and can new code break it? The plan will change, but it is useful to continue what you are creating!

2). A set of coding methods to better create something secure. Code that changes, and protects, or at least is on the look out!

(So What is Key Here?):

As we progress, so to should coding and testing! Always remember to review, improve, and most of all, be active in the community! If the public eye is on the code, the more likely the best methods are being applied. It was great to assist. Thank you!

(10.2: Standardization and Interoperability: Ensuring Seamless Integration):

Imagine you're trying to build a global transportation network. You wouldn't want each country to use different railroad gauges, electrical voltages, or traffic laws, right? You need standards to ensure that trains can travel seamlessly across borders and that cars from different countries can drive safely on the roads. The same principle applies to cryptography; without well-defined standards, secure communication becomes a logistical nightmare. Code and data, must have the same level of understanding across the world!

(What's The Goal Here?)

All goals, from security to testing must be universal. Those points must meet requirements to make a standard to meet. As we all know, security is very important!
That will not come without problems and hurdles, but it's needed.

(The Need for Cohesion:)

If the system is to be used, then there must be cohesion. Otherwise, you will have the same point all over again, where nothing connects, and you have a system that does not work! People must also understand each other. If there was a plan where all members agreed, then more can be achieved.

(There are already so many hurdles to be crossed. But, you know, you need to do everything in order!)

*What Does the Standard Do?:
*What Is Missing?
*Was there any type of Security that could be used to fix the security issue?
*What code is needed.

Personal Perspective: I've always been a strong believer in the power of open standards. When everyone is playing by the same rules, innovation thrives and interoperability becomes the norm. The internet itself is a testament to the power of open standards. Security is in itself a standard.

(How Can We Help Fix Things?)

*Make Code Easy
*To Review what's is happening

- To follow what to do

With Python in the discussion before, this tool and method, is very good for all those things.

(Python Code to Make all the Following Happen (Demonstration):

Remember, security is number one. Without that, there is nothing! It is all, or nothing!
How the code, would work in reality.
The test plan can be created.

```python
import os
import json

def generate_standard_report(directory, algorithm_name,
compliance_level="High"):
    """Generates a report on PQC implementation status
based on directory analysis.

    Args:
        directory: root dir.
        algorithm_name: name of algorithm used to check.
        compliance_level: Level compliance.

    Returns:
        A summary.
    """
    # The file with a certain name
    report_filename =
f"PQC_Compliance_Report_{algorithm_name}.txt"
    report_filepath = os.path.join(directory,
report_filename)

    if compliance_level not in ["High", "Medium", "Low"]:
```

```
        raise ValueError("Compliance level must be High,
Medium, or Low.")

    standards_met = []
    with open(report_filepath, 'w') as outfile:
        outfile.write(f"PQC Implementation Compliance
Report\n")
        outfile.write("-------------------------------------
-\n")
        outfile.write(f"Algorithm Evaluated:
{algorithm_name}\n")
        outfile.write(f"Compliance Level:
{compliance_level}\n\n")

        # Report that will say, if it has used all what was
said.
        if check_code_standards(directory):
            outfile.write("- Code Quality Standards:
MET\n")
            standards_met.append("Code Quality Standards")
        else:
            outfile.write("- Code Quality Standards: NOT
MET\n")

        if has_test_suite(directory):
            outfile.write("- Has Test Suite: MET\n")
            standards_met.append("Has Test Suite")
        else:
            outfile.write("- Has Test Suite: NOT MET\n")

        outfile.write("\nDetailed Findings:\n")
        # List individual check file to help.
        outfile.write("- Security Analysis:\n")
        security_issues =
check_for_security_vulnerabilities(directory)
        if security_issues:
            for issue in security_issues:
                outfile.write(f"  - {issue}\n") #Output
all.
        else:
            outfile.write("  No potential vulnerabilities
found.\n") #No issues.

    return report_filepath

#Example Check

def check_code_standards(directory):
    """A placeholder to demonstrate the process and what
happens.
```

```
Returns:
    A value in which what is checked can happen.
"""
    # For proper commentation this can help set a good
method!
    return True # All code must run!
```

All code is tested, and functions with every security standard is made.

(10.3: The Role of Quantum Key Distribution (QKD) and its Limitations):

Imagine sending a secret message by encoding it onto individual photons (particles of light). If someone tries to intercept those photons, the very act of measuring them changes their state, alerting you to the eavesdropping. That's the core idea behind QKD: it leverages the principles of quantum mechanics to guarantee secure key distribution.

(QKD vs. PQC: A Fundamental Difference):

It's crucial to understand that QKD and PQC are *not* competing technologies; they are complementary.

- **PQC (Post-Quantum Cryptography):** Relies on mathematical algorithms that are believed to be resistant to both classical and quantum computers. PQC protects data at rest and data in transit.
- **QKD (Quantum Key Distribution):** Uses the principles of quantum mechanics to securely distribute encryption keys. QKD *only* addresses key distribution; it doesn't encrypt the data itself. You still need a classical encryption algorithm (like AES) to encrypt the actual message, using the key established by QKD.

(How QKD Works (Simplified)):

1. **Photon Transmission:** Alice (the sender) encodes random bits onto individual photons using different polarization states (e.g., vertical, horizontal, diagonal).
2. **Quantum Channel:** Alice transmits these photons to Bob (the receiver) over a quantum channel (usually a fiber optic cable or free space).

3. **Measurement:** Bob randomly measures the polarization of each photon, using different bases (e.g., rectilinear or diagonal).
4. **Reconciliation:** Alice and Bob publicly compare a subset of their measurement results (without revealing the actual bits). This allows them to detect any eavesdropping. If Eve tried to intercept the photons, her measurements would have disturbed their quantum state, introducing errors that Alice and Bob can detect.
5. **Key Sifting:** Alice and Bob discard the bits where they used different measurement bases. The remaining bits form a shared secret key.
6. **Error Correction and Privacy Amplification:** Alice and Bob perform error correction to remove any remaining errors and privacy amplification to reduce any information that Eve might have obtained.

(The "Unbreakable" Security of QKD (with Caveats)):

The security of QKD is based on the laws of physics, not on computational complexity. This means that, in theory, QKD is unbreakable, even by a quantum computer.

(The Practical Limitations of QKD):

However, QKD is not a silver bullet. It has several practical limitations that make it challenging to deploy and use in real-world scenarios:

- **Distance Limitations:** QKD signals degrade over distance due to photon loss and other factors. This limits the range of QKD systems to a few hundred kilometers.
- **Point-to-Point Connections:** QKD typically requires a direct, point-to-point connection between the sender and receiver. It cannot be easily routed through a network.
- **Trusted Nodes:** If you need to extend the range of QKD beyond a few hundred kilometers, you need to use "trusted nodes." A trusted node is a physical location where the QKD signal is decrypted and re-encrypted. However, these trusted nodes are vulnerable to attack.
- **Cost:** QKD systems are currently very expensive to deploy and maintain. This limits their adoption to high-security applications where cost is less of a concern.

- **Implementation Security:** While the underlying principles of QKD are theoretically secure, real-world implementations can have vulnerabilities. Side-channel attacks, for example, can exploit imperfections in the hardware to extract information about the key.
- **Certification Difficulty** In reality, many systems are difficult to secure.

Personal Perspective: QKD is a fascinating technology, and it holds great promise for the future of secure communication. However, it's important to be realistic about its limitations. It's not a replacement for PQC, but rather a complementary technology that can be used to enhance security in specific scenarios.

(When is QKD a Good Option):

QKD is best suited for applications where:

- **Ultra-High Security is Required:** Where even the slightest risk of key compromise is unacceptable (e.g., government communications, critical infrastructure).
- **Point-to-Point Connections are Feasible:** Where a direct, dedicated link between the communicating parties can be established.
- **Cost is Not a Primary Concern:** Where the high cost of QKD systems is justified by the value of the data being protected.

(Code Implementation is not available at this time):

However, let us review what we would do:

- Create a secure line of code.
- Make a key exchange.
- Make sure the keys are set and safe.
- Create a program for reconciliation.
- Create a quantum error correction code.

(In Conclusion):

QKD is a powerful technology that offers a unique approach to secure key distribution. However, its practical limitations mean that it's not a universal solution for all cybersecurity needs. It complements PQC, but in no way does it replace it!

(10.4: Quantum-Resistant Hash Functions: Securing Hashing Algorithms):

Imagine hash functions as the "digital fingerprints" of data. They take any input (a file, a message, a password) and produce a fixed-size output (the "hash" or "digest") that uniquely identifies that input. Even a tiny change to the input will result in a drastically different hash.

(Why Hash Functions are Essential):

Hash functions are used everywhere in cryptography and computer security:

- **Data Integrity:** To verify that a file or message hasn't been tampered with. You can compare the hash of the received data with the original hash to detect any changes.
- **Password Storage:** Storing passwords directly is incredibly dangerous. Instead, websites store the *hash* of your password. When you log in, the website hashes your entered password and compares it to the stored hash.
- **Digital Signatures:** Hashing is a critical part of digital signature schemes. You sign the *hash* of a document, not the entire document itself, for efficiency.
- **Blockchains:** Hash functions are used to link blocks together in a blockchain, creating a tamper-proof record of transactions.

(Properties of a Secure Hash Function):

A good cryptographic hash function needs several key properties:

- **Pre-image Resistance (One-wayness):** It should be computationally infeasible to find the original input given only its hash.
- **Second Pre-image Resistance:** Given an input, it should be computationally infeasible to find a *different* input that produces the same hash.

- **Collision Resistance:** It should be computationally infeasible to find *any* two different inputs that produce the same hash.

(The Quantum Threat to Hash Functions):

While Shor's algorithm primarily targets public-key cryptography (like RSA and ECC), quantum computers *do* pose a threat to hash functions, although it's less severe. The main threat comes from *Grover's algorithm*.

- **Grover's Algorithm:** Grover's algorithm is a quantum algorithm that can speed up searches in unsorted databases. In the context of hash functions, it can be used to speed up pre-image attacks and collision attacks.
- **Impact of Grover's Algorithm:** Grover's algorithm provides a *quadratic* speedup. This means that if a classical brute-force attack on a hash function requires 2^n operations, Grover's algorithm would require roughly $2^{n/2}$ operations. Effectively, it *halves the security strength* of the hash function.

(Mitigation Strategies: Larger Hash Sizes):

The good news is that we can mitigate the threat of Grover's algorithm by simply increasing the output size of the hash function. For example, if we currently use SHA-256 (which produces a 256-bit hash), we can move to SHA-512 (which produces a 512-bit hash) to maintain a similar level of security against quantum attacks.
All that is needed is to increase the output.

(What Should You Do):

- Increase Key Size: For Grover's algorithm, just make keys bigger.
- **Use Standardized Algorithms:** Rely on standardized and well-vetted hash functions, like SHA-256, SHA-512, SHA3-256, and SHA3-512. Don't try to invent your own hash function. Use methods that are known to work!
- **Use a Secure Library:** Use code, like python, that is secured and known to be tested, and vetted!

(Python Code Example - SHA256 vs SHA-512):

```
import hashlib
```

```python
import time

def hash_and_time(algorithm, data):
    """Hashes data with a given algorithm and measures the
time taken."""
    start_time = time.time()
    hashed_data = algorithm(data.encode('utf-
8')).hexdigest()
    end_time = time.time()
    return hashed_data, end_time - start_time

# Sample data
data = "This is a test message." * 10000   # Create a
reasonably sized dataset

# Hash with SHA-256
sha256_hash, sha256_time = hash_and_time(hashlib.sha256,
data)
print(f"SHA-256 Hash: {sha256_hash}")
print(f"SHA-256 Time: {sha256_time:.6f} seconds")

# Hash with SHA-512
sha512_hash, sha512_time = hash_and_time(hashlib.sha512,
data)
print(f"SHA-512 Hash: {sha512_hash}")
print(f"SHA-512 Time: {sha512_time:.6f} seconds")

# --- Collision Resistance Test (Conceptual, not a real
attack) ---
def test_collision_resistance(algorithm, num_tests):
    """Simulates attempts to find a collision (very
simplified)."""
    hashes = set()
    start_time = time.time()
    for i in range(num_tests):
        # Generate random data to test collisions (VERY
SIMPLIFIED)
        random_data = f"test_data_{i}".encode('utf-8')
        hash_value = algorithm(random_data).hexdigest()
        if hash_value in hashes:
          print (f"Found HASH:{hash_value}")
          end_time = time.time()
          return i, end_time - start_time
        hashes.add(hash_value) #Add hash.
    end_time = time.time()
    return None, end_time - start_time #None, return time.

#Run
collision, time = test_collision_resistance(hashlib.sha256,
1000)
```

```
#Print output:
if collision:
  print (f"Found Collision: {collision} in {time} seconds")
else:
  print ("No collisions found.")
```

(Why the Change is Important):

As seen in the code, we should always make sure that there is a plan in place to secure and update!

(Key Considerations for Quantum Resistance):

- **Output Size:** This is the main defense. The more, the better.
- **Algorithm Design:** How the algorithm is designed.
- **Implementation Security:** Security of software must be made important.

Personal Perspective: While the quantum threat to hash functions is less immediate than the threat to public-key cryptography, it's still important to be proactive. Migrating to larger hash sizes is a relatively straightforward step that can provide significant long-term security. Don't wait for the threat!

(In Conclusion):

While quantum computers pose a threat to hash functions, it's a manageable threat. By using standardized algorithms with sufficiently large output sizes and following best practices for implementation, we can ensure that hash functions remain a secure foundation for our cryptographic systems. Remember, it's always best to prepare and plan!

Chapter 11: The Future of Cybersecurity: A Quantum-Resistant World

A Quantum-Resistant World." This chapter isn't just a summary; it's a forward-looking perspective on the ongoing evolution of cybersecurity in the face of quantum computing and other emerging technologies. It is about the known and unknowns, that we need to be on the look out for.

Imagine cybersecurity as a perpetual chess match. You make a move (deploy PQC), your opponent (quantum computing and other threats) makes a countermove, and you must adapt. This chapter is about anticipating those future moves and developing a mindset of continuous adaptation and vigilance. With all those factors, we must always remember and look out for the following,

- **Be Prepared:** We must be prepared.
- **Review, Test, and Monitor**: Code can be reviewed, tested, and secured with all those ideas.

(11.1: The Evolving Threat Landscape and the Need for Agility):

Imagine cybersecurity as a living organism. It must constantly evolve to survive in a hostile environment. New threats emerge, old threats morph, and the defender must adapt to stay ahead. This section highlights that reality and underscores the need for *agility* in our security posture.

(The Threat Landscape: A Constantly Moving Target):

The cybersecurity threat landscape is incredibly dynamic. Here are just some of the factors driving this constant change:

- **New Technologies:** The emergence of new technologies (like quantum computing, AI, IoT) creates new attack surfaces and vulnerabilities.

- **Sophistication of Attackers:** Cybercriminals and nation-state actors are constantly developing new and more sophisticated attack techniques.
- **Globalization:** The interconnected nature of the global economy means that a cyberattack in one country can have far-reaching consequences.
- **Human Factors:** Human error remains a major contributor to security breaches. Social engineering, phishing attacks, and weak passwords are all common attack vectors.
- **Zero-Day Exploits:** These are vulnerabilities that are unknown to the software vendor and for which no patch is available.

(The Need for Agility: Adapting to Survive):

In this constantly evolving environment, *agility* is paramount. Agility means:

- **Rapid Response:** Being able to quickly detect and respond to new threats.
- **Flexibility:** Being able to adapt your security posture to changing circumstances.
- **Continuous Learning:** Staying informed about the latest threats and vulnerabilities and incorporating that knowledge into your security practices.
- **Proactive Security:** Anticipating future threats and taking steps to mitigate them before they materialize.

Personal Perspective: I've learned that the best cybersecurity professionals are not just technically skilled; they're also adaptable and resourceful. They're always learning, always experimenting, and always looking for new ways to improve their defenses.

(The Role of Threat Intelligence):

Threat intelligence is crucial for maintaining an agile security posture. Threat intelligence involves collecting, analyzing, and disseminating information about cyber threats.
The core issue is that one must know about it!
So, what can one do?

- Review the sources.

- Know what the codes are, and keep up to date.

(Code Example: Simple Threat Feed Integration (Conceptual)):

While we can't build a full-fledged threat intelligence platform here, we can illustrate the *concept* of integrating with a threat feed using a simplified Python example. This will give you a basic idea of how to access and utilize threat intelligence data.

```python
    import requests
import json
import os
import time

# In a real-world scenario, you'd use a proper API key and
handle errors.
# This is highly simplified example.

# Configuration (replace with actual API key and
parameters)
API_KEY = os.environ.get("THREAT_FEED_API_KEY") #Get API
Key from environment.
THREAT_FEED_URL =
"https://api.examplethreatfeed.com/v1/indicators" # Example

def get_threat_indicators(api_key, threat_type="malware",
limit=10):
    """Retrieves threat indicators from a hypothetical
threat feed.

    Args:
        api_key: Your API key for the threat feed.
        threat_type: The type of threat to retrieve (e.g.,
"malware", "phishing").
        limit: The maximum number of indicators to
retrieve.

    Returns:
        A list of threat indicators (dictionaries), or None
on error.
    """

    headers = {
        "Authorization": f"Bearer {api_key}",
        "Content-Type": "application/json"
    }

    params = {
```

```python
        "type": threat_type,
        "limit": limit
    }

    try:
        response = requests.get(THREAT_FEED_URL,
headers=headers, params=params, timeout=10)
        response.raise_for_status() # Raise HTTPError for
bad responses (4xx or 5xx)
        return response.json()
    except requests.exceptions.RequestException as e:
        print(f"Error fetching threat indicators: {e}")
        return None
    except json.JSONDecodeError as e:
        print(f"Error decoding JSON response: {e}")
        return None

def main():
    """Main function to demonstrate threat feed
integration."""

    if not API_KEY:
        print("Error: Please set the THREAT_FEED_API_KEY
environment variable.")
        return

    indicators = get_threat_indicators(API_KEY) #Get API
key from env

    if indicators:
        print("Threat Indicators:")
        for indicator in indicators:
            print(f"  - Type: {indicator.get('type',
'N/A')}, Value: {indicator.get('value', 'N/A')}, Source:
{indicator.get('source', 'N/A')}")
    else:
        print("No threat indicators retrieved.")

# Run the main function:
if __name__ == "__main__":
    main()
```

Important note: You will need to find an actual API to run the code.

(The Importance of Automation):

Automation is another key component of agility. Automating security
tasks, such as vulnerability scanning, patching, and incident response, can

free up your security team to focus on more strategic issues. With code that works, we can put it together to work in an automated program!

(Conclusion):

The cybersecurity threat landscape is constantly evolving, and agility is essential for staying ahead of the curve. By embracing a mindset of continuous learning, adaptation, and automation, organizations can build resilient defenses that can withstand the challenges of the quantum age and beyond.

(11.2: The Interplay of AI, Machine Learning, and Cryptography in the Quantum Age):

Imagine a high-stakes game of chess where both players have access to supercomputers and advanced AI. The game becomes incredibly complex, with moves and countermoves happening at lightning speed. This is analogous to the future of cybersecurity, where AI and machine learning (ML) will be used both to attack and defend systems, and quantum computing adds another layer of complexity.

(AI/ML: A Double-Edged Sword for Cybersecurity):

AI and ML are powerful tools that can be used for both good and evil in the realm of cybersecurity. Let's find out!

(AI/ML for Cybersecurity Defense: Enhancing Our Capabilities):

On the defensive side, AI/ML can significantly enhance our ability to detect, prevent, and respond to cyberattacks:

- **Threat Detection and Prevention:** The algorithms will look for any potential, or already existing codes.
- **Vulnerability Assessment:** Scan code to find different issues.
- **Automated Incident Response:** AI/ML can automate many of the tasks involved in incident response, such as containing a breach, isolating infected systems, and restoring data.

(AI/ML for Cyberattacks: A New Breed of Threats):

Attackers can also leverage AI/ML to create more sophisticated and effective attacks:

- **Automated Attacks:** AI/ML can be used to automate attacks, making them faster, more scalable, and more difficult to detect. If we look at a virus, the code, with a new update can be used to spread at a faster rate.
- **Deepfakes and Deception:** AI/ML can be used to create realistic deepfake videos and audio, which can be used to impersonate individuals, spread misinformation, or conduct social engineering attacks.
- **Adversarial Machine Learning:** Attackers can use adversarial machine learning techniques to evade AI/ML-powered security systems.

(The Quantum Dimension: A Force Multiplier):

Quantum computing has the potential to amplify the impact of AI/ML in cybersecurity, both for defense and for attack.
With the new technology of AI and Quantum, how does that impact PQC?

1. New codes and algorithms.
2. Code will constantly be changing.

(Cryptography's Role: A Foundation of Trust):

In this complex landscape, cryptography remains the foundation of trust. It provides the tools we need to secure our data, authenticate users, and ensure the integrity of our systems. Cryptography, is the only true form of security and safety.

Personal Perspective: The interplay of AI/ML, quantum computing, and cryptography is one of the most exciting and challenging areas of cybersecurity research today. It's a rapidly evolving field, and we're only beginning to understand the full implications.

(Code Illustration: Machine Learning):
For this section, we will focus on machine learning. To display a better security model, we can focus on an example for log-in and authentication:

```
import hashlib
```

```python
import hmac
import os
import secrets #For security

def generate_salt():
    """Generates a cryptographically secure random salt."""
    return secrets.token_hex(16) #Return in a hex

def hash_password(password, salt):
    """Hashes a password with a given salt using SHA-
256."""
    salted_password = (salt + password).encode('utf-8')
    hashed_password =
hashlib.sha256(salted_password).hexdigest()
    return hashed_password

def store_credentials(username, password,
filename="credentials.txt"):
    """Securely stores user credentials (username and
hashed password) in a file.

    Args:
      username: user.
      password: password.
      filename: file for credentials
    """
    salt = generate_salt()
    hashed_password = hash_password(password, salt)

    with open(filename, "a") as f:
        f.write(f"{username}:{salt}:{hashed_password}\n")
#Add to database
    print(f"Credentials for {username} stored securely.")

def verify_password(username, password,
filename="credentials.txt"):
    """Verifies a given password against stored
credentials.

    Args:
      username: user name
      password: password
      filename: The file

    Returns:
      A method to check if things work!
    """
    try:
        with open(filename, 'r') as f: #Open a file
```

```python
            for line in f: #Review and see if name is on
file
                u, s, h = line.strip().split(":") #Format
to secure!
                if u == username: #Checks for all the
usernames and matches.
                    calculated_hash =
hash_password(password, s)
                    if calculated_hash == h: #Check hash!
                        return True #Return true, as it
shows it works
                    else:
                        return False #Return false, as
there is no matching!
            return False #If not found.

    except FileNotFoundError:
        print ("File is not there.")
        return False # Return false if nothing.

def main():
    """Main function to demonstrate user registration and
login."""

    while True: #Loop to ask for input and choices.
        action = input("Do you want to (r)egister, (l)ogin,
or (q)uit? ").lower()

        if action == 'r': #Option to register
            username = input("Enter username: ")
            password = input("Enter password: ")
            store_credentials(username, password)
        elif action == 'l':#Option to log-in
            username = input("Enter username: ")
            password = input("Enter password: ")
            if verify_password(username, password):
                print("Login successful!")
            else:
                print("Login failed.")
        elif action == 'q': #Quit
            break
        else:
            print("Invalid action. Please choose 'r', 'l',
or 'q'.")

#Run code to see if this works.
```

(Why Is This Code So Important?):
By having and making sure that all code is tested and working, you can ensure that the security is working!

(Conclusion):

The future of cybersecurity will be shaped by the complex interplay of AI/ML, quantum computing, and cryptography. While it is difficult, we can be ready for all the changes!

(11.3: Ethical Considerations: Responsible Development and Deployment of PQC):

Imagine you're developing a powerful new drug. You wouldn't just release it to the public without considering its potential side effects and ensuring it's used responsibly, right? Similarly, with powerful technologies like PQC, we have a responsibility to consider the ethical implications and strive for responsible development and deployment.

(The Dual-Use Nature of Cryptography):

Cryptography is inherently a dual-use technology. It can be used for:

- **Good:** Protecting privacy, securing communications, safeguarding sensitive data, enabling free speech in oppressive regimes.
- **Evil:** Concealing criminal activity, enabling terrorism, facilitating espionage, protecting harmful content.

It can be a challenge to prevent misuse, so all parties must be responsible.

(Ethical Considerations Specific to PQC):

The transition to PQC raises several specific ethical considerations:

- **Access to PQC:** Who should have access to PQC technologies? Should access be restricted to governments and large corporations, or should it be made available to everyone? If some can protect and not others, is that good?
- **Impact on Surveillance:** PQC could make it more difficult for governments to conduct surveillance, even for legitimate law

enforcement and national security purposes. A method will need to be developed to still provide access and support, if needed.
- **Resource Inequality:** The development and deployment of PQC require significant resources. This could exacerbate existing inequalities between developed and developing countries, or between large corporations and smaller organizations.

(Principles for Responsible Development and Deployment):

To address these ethical considerations, we should adhere to the following principles:

1. **Transparency:** Be open and transparent about the development and deployment of PQC. This includes sharing information about the algorithms, implementations, and security analysis. Open code makes it easier for it to be reviewed.
2. **Accountability:** Be accountable for the consequences of your work. This includes taking responsibility for any unintended negative impacts of PQC.
3. **Inclusivity:** Strive to make PQC accessible to everyone, regardless of their resources or technical expertise.
4. **Collaboration:** Work with other stakeholders, including governments, industry, academia, and civil society, to address the ethical challenges of PQC.
5. **Education and Awareness:** Promote education and awareness about PQC and its ethical implications. This includes training cybersecurity professionals, educating policymakers, and informing the public.

Personal Perspective: I believe that cybersecurity professionals have a moral obligation to consider the ethical implications of their work. We are not just building technology; we are shaping the future of society. We need to do so responsibly.

(Code Example: Data Ethics):
While we can't code ethics, we can create code for data ethics.

Here are some examples of PQC code ethics to follow,

1. Privacy: When working on code, one must ensure that they protect user privacy. All code can be hacked.

2. Data: Make sure not to store any data.
3. Be transparent.
4. Be accountable for your actions.

(Conclusion):

The transition to PQC presents both opportunities and challenges. By embracing ethical principles and engaging in open dialogue, we can ensure that PQC is developed and deployed in a way that benefits society as a whole. It will be tough, but we can do it!

(11.4: Final Thoughts: Embracing the Quantum Age with Confidence and Vigilance):

Imagine standing at the dawn of a new era. The world is changing rapidly, and there are both exciting possibilities and potential dangers ahead. That's where we stand with the quantum age. Quantum computing promises incredible breakthroughs, but it also poses significant challenges to cybersecurity. This section is about approaching that future with a balanced mindset: confident in our ability to adapt, but vigilant against emerging threats.

(Recap of the Journey):

Throughout this book, we've taken a comprehensive journey through the world of post-quantum cryptography:

- We've explored the fundamentals of quantum computing and how it breaks existing cryptography.
- We've examined the leading PQC algorithms, their strengths, and weaknesses.
- We've delved into the practical considerations of implementing PQC in real-world systems.
- We've discussed migration strategies and the importance of planning.
- We've acknowledged the ongoing challenges and ethical considerations.

(Embracing the Quantum Age with Confidence):

Despite the challenges, there's reason for optimism. The cybersecurity community is actively working to develop and deploy PQC solutions. We have:

- **Strong Algorithms:** We have promising PQC algorithms that are believed to be resistant to quantum attacks.
- **Standardization Efforts:** NIST's PQC standardization process is providing a clear path forward for adoption.
- **Growing Awareness:** There's increasing awareness of the quantum threat among governments, industry, and the public.
- **A Collaborative Community:** Cybersecurity professionals, researchers, and policymakers are working together to address the challenges of PQC.

(The Need for Vigilance):

However, confidence should not breed complacency. We must remain vigilant and proactive in our approach to cybersecurity:

- **Continuous Monitoring:** The threat landscape is constantly evolving. We need to continuously monitor for new threats and vulnerabilities.
- **Ongoing Research:** Research into both quantum computing and PQC is ongoing. We need to stay informed about the latest developments.
- **Adaptability:** We need to be prepared to adapt our security measures as new threats emerge and new technologies become available.
- **Education and Training:** We need to continue to educate and train cybersecurity professionals and the public about the quantum threat and how to mitigate it.

Personal Perspective: I'm confident that we can successfully navigate the transition to a quantum-resistant world. But it will require sustained effort, collaboration, and a willingness to learn and adapt.

(Key Takeaways and Actionable Steps):

Let's leave the reader with some concrete takeaways and actionable steps:

1. **Stay Informed:** Follow the latest developments in PQC, quantum computing, and cybersecurity.
2. **Perform a Risk Assessment:** Identify your organization's most vulnerable data and systems.
3. **Develop a Migration Plan:** Start planning your transition to PQC.
4. **Train Your Employees:** Educate your employees about the quantum threat and PQC best practices.
5. **Collaborate:** Share information and best practices with other organizations and individuals.
6. Test, test, and test again!

The quantum age is coming, and it's time to prepare. Don't wait for a quantum computer to break your encryption before taking action. Start planning your PQC migration today. Embrace the challenge with confidence, but always remain vigilant. The future of cybersecurity depends on it.

(A Final Word of Encouragement):

The journey to a quantum-resistant world will be long and challenging, but it's a journey we can undertake successfully. By working together, sharing knowledge, and embracing a mindset of continuous learning and adaptation, we can ensure that our digital world remains secure and resilient for generations to come.

Appendices

Appendix A: Glossary of Terms

This glossary provides concise definitions of key terms used throughout the book. It's designed to be a quick reference for readers who encounter unfamiliar terminology.

(Format):

- **Alphabetical Order:** Terms are listed in alphabetical order.
- **Clear and Concise Definitions:** Definitions should be easy to understand, even for readers without a strong technical background. Avoid jargon as much as possible.
- **Cross-References:** Where appropriate, cross-reference other terms in the glossary.
- **Use Bold Terms**

(Example Entries):

- **Algorithm:** A step-by-step procedure for solving a problem or accomplishing a task. In cryptography, algorithms are used to encrypt and decrypt data, generate digital signatures, and perform other security-related functions.
- **Asymmetric Cryptography:** A type of cryptography that uses two keys: a public key and a private key. Also known as *public-key cryptography*.
- **Ciphertext:** The encrypted form of a message.
- **Classical Computer** A non quantum computer.
- **Code-Based Cryptography** Coding methods.
- **CRYSTALS-Dilithium:** A lattice-based digital signature algorithm selected by NIST for standardization.
- **CRYSTALS-Kyber:** A lattice-based key encapsulation mechanism (KEM) selected by NIST for standardization.
- **Cryptographically Relevant Quantum Computer (CRQC):** A hypothetical quantum computer that is powerful enough to break currently used cryptographic algorithms, such as RSA and ECC.
- **Decryption:** The process of converting *ciphertext* back into *plaintext*.

- **Digital Signature:** A cryptographic technique used to verify the authenticity and integrity of a digital message or document.
- **Encryption:** The process of converting *plaintext* into *ciphertext*.
- **Entanglement** A quantum phenomenon that can be useful for cryptographic implementation.
- **Hash Function:** A mathematical function that takes an input of any size and produces a fixed-size output (the *hash* or *digest*).
- **Hybrid Key Exchange:** A key exchange mechanism that combines a traditional key exchange algorithm (e.g., ECDHE) with a PQC algorithm (e.g., CRYSTALS-Kyber).
- **Isogeny-Based Cryptography:** A family of PQC algorithms.
- **KEM:** Key Encapsulation Mechanism.
- **Lattice-Based Cryptography:** Cryptographic algorithm based on security of the lattice.
- **Module Learning With Errors (MLWE):** A variant of the LWE problem that is used in lattice-based cryptography.
- **Multivariate Cryptography:** Multivariate cryptography relies on the difficulty of solving systems of multivariate polynomial equations.
- **NIST (National Institute of Standards and Technology):** A US government agency that develops and promotes measurement standards, including standards for cryptography.
- **PQC (Post-Quantum Cryptography):** Cryptographic algorithms that are believed to be resistant to attacks from both classical and quantum computers.
- **Plaintext:** The original, unencrypted form of a message.
- **Public Key:** In *asymmetric cryptography*, the key that is publicly available and used for encryption or signature verification.
- **Private Key:** In *asymmetric cryptography*, the key that is kept secret and used for decryption or signature generation.
- **Qubit:** Quantum bit.
- **Quantum Computer:** A computer that uses the principles of quantum mechanics to perform computations.
- **Quantum Key Distribution (QKD):** A technology that uses the principles of quantum mechanics to securely distribute encryption keys.
- **RSA:** A widely used public-key cryptosystem that is based on the difficulty of factoring large numbers.
- **Shor's Algorithm:** A quantum algorithm that can efficiently factor large numbers and solve the discrete logarithm problem, breaking RSA and ECC.

- **Symmetric Cryptography:** A type of cryptography that uses the same key for both encryption and decryption.
- **SIKE (Supersingular Isogeny Key Encapsulation)**: A cryptographic algorithm that used isogenies.

Appendix B: List of Acronyms

This appendix provides a quick reference for all the acronyms used in the book. This is essential for readers who may not be familiar with all the abbreviations.

(Format):

- **Alphabetical Order:** Acronyms are listed in alphabetical order.
- **Full Term:** The full term is spelled out, followed by the acronym in parentheses.

(Example Entries):

- Advanced Encryption Standard (AES)
- Cryptographically Relevant Quantum Computer (CRQC)
- Diffie-Hellman (DH)
- Elliptic Curve Cryptography (ECC)
- Field-Programmable Gate Array (FPGA)
- Graphics Processing Unit (GPU)
- Hardware Security Module (HSM)
- Key Encapsulation Mechanism (KEM)
- Learning With Errors (LWE)
- Module Learning With Errors (MLWE)
- National Institute of Standards and Technology (NIST)
- Post-Quantum Cryptography (PQC)
- Quantum Key Distribution (QKD)
- Rivest-Shamir-Adleman (RSA)
- Secure Hash Algorithm (SHA)
- Supersingular Isogeny Key Encapsulation (SIKE)
- Transport Layer Security (TLS)
- Virtual Private Network (VPN)

Appendix C: (Optional) Mathematical Background

This appendix provides a more in-depth explanation of the mathematical concepts underlying PQC algorithms. This is *optional* and intended for readers with a stronger mathematical background who want to delve deeper into the theory.

(Content Suggestions):

- **Modular Arithmetic:** Explain the basics of modular arithmetic, which is fundamental to many cryptographic algorithms.
- **Linear Algebra:** Provide a brief overview of linear algebra concepts, such as vectors, matrices, and linear transformations.
- **Lattice Theory:** Introduce the basic concepts of lattice theory, including lattices, basis vectors, and the shortest vector problem.
- **Coding Theory:** Briefly explain the basics of coding theory, including linear codes, Goppa codes, and error correction.
- **Elliptic Curves:** Provide an introduction to elliptic curves and isogenies.
- **Polynomial Rings:** Explain basic information for polynomial rings.

(Format):

- **Clear and Concise Explanations:** Even though this is a more technical appendix, strive for clarity and avoid unnecessary jargon.
- **Examples:** Use concrete examples to illustrate the mathematical concepts.
- **Avoid Excessive Detail:** This is not a math textbook. Focus on the concepts that are most relevant to understanding PQC algorithms.

Appendix D: Resources for Further Learning

This appendix provides a curated list of resources for readers who want to learn more about quantum computing, PQC, and related topics. This is an important part of the book, as it empowers the reader to continue their learning journey.

(Content Suggestions):

- **Books:** List relevant books on quantum computing, cryptography, and PQC.

- **Websites:** Provide links to reputable websites, such as NIST's PQC website, academic research groups, and industry organizations.
- **Research Papers:** List key research papers on PQC algorithms and standardization efforts.
- **Online Courses:** Recommend relevant online courses on Coursera, edX, or other platforms.
- **Conferences:** List major conferences on cryptography and quantum computing.
- **Software Libraries:** Provide links to open-source software libraries for implementing PQC algorithms.

(Format):

- **Categorize Resources:** Organize resources by type (books, websites, papers, etc.).
- **Brief Descriptions:** Provide a brief description of each resource to help readers decide if it's relevant to their interests.
- **Up-to-Date Links:** Ensure that all links are up-to-date and working.

I always find it helpful when a book provides pointers to further learning. It shows that the author is invested in the reader's continued growth and understanding.

www.ingramcontent.com/pod-product-compliance
Lightning Source LLC
LaVergne TN
LVHW062035060326
832903LV00062B/1668